CLASSIC
SAILING YACHTS

WHITE STAR PUBLISHERS

CONTENTS

TEXT Jill Bobrow

PROJECT EDITOR Valeria Manferto De Fabianis

EDITORIAL ASSISTANTS Giorgia Raineri - Giorgio Ferrero

GRAPHIC DESIGN Paola Piacco

INTRODUCTION

*S*ometime in the early 1940s, Captain Arthur "Chummy" Spurling of Great Cranberry Island, Maine, started building rowing skiffs. He built them the time-honored way, by eye and by feel, each vessel a subtle evolution of the previous one – a bit more hollow at the waterline forward, or perhaps the merest extra kick to the sheer aft. They were a delight to row and a pleasure to look at, whether pulled up on a dock where they could display their lines or, as was typically the case, towed behind a larger yacht.

Chummy's skiffs, by any definition, were yachts. They were certainly more than just tenders. In an era when people went rowing for the pleasure of it; they were unfailingly graceful, without a discordant note in their lines. Beauty and performance – add, in appropriate proportions, wood, varnish, bronze and a hint of leather chafing gear and we have the definition of a classic yacht.

In almost every way, Chummy's little rowboats are the perfect paradigm for the sequence of events that allows us today to take pleasure in an astonishing diversity of classic yachts, to enjoy them as owners, sailors or as appreciative spectators from a distance. Those little skiffs were built using traditional methods and materials. Sadly, many were eventually neglected as their owners' interests changed or the increasing cost of maintenance caused them to be replaced by mass-produced fiberglass dinghies. Some were simply damaged and lost, but several continued to be cherished and lovingly maintained. Today, you can buy a fiberglass version of a Spurling skiff or, for a substantial price, have a wooden replica built.

The same holds true of almost any classic yacht. Before we continue, we must take up the challenge of defining, within the context of yachts and yachting, that vexing term that will become all too familiar within the pages that follow: "classic."

Considering that almost everything (other than actual specifications) related to the yachts in these pages is subjective, is it really possible to have a rational discussion of whether William Fife or Nathanael Herreshoff designed prettier boats? Or, for that matter, which one built better boats? Perhaps we should initially settle upon the one description of a classic yacht that succeeds when all else fails: "I know one when I see one." After all is said and done, this is a perfectly valid starting point. We can have an ongoing dialogue about the correct curve for a proper sheerline or where the break in the perfect spoon bow should occur and never agree. But whatever our individual preference, we still all recognize – and turn around to look at – a graceful classic yacht and are united in our common love for what she represents.

It is essential, however, not to let romanticism and sentimentality cloud our thinking. The classic yachts in question have become cherished possessions and have changed from being mere sailing craft that were loved and enjoyed to their current status as emotional and financial commitments (and not necessarily rational ones at that). And those who sail them are no longer mere sailors but are part of a select coterie. They have become a sort of sub-species of the genus "sailor" for whom the boats are no longer just another sport but have become a passion. And passion, while it can be channeled into a positive and constructive energy, can also blind us.

1 MARIQUITA, MOONBEAM III, AND LULWORTH PRESENT A NOSTALGIC PICTURE FOR ALL LOVERS OF CLASSIC SAILING YACHTS.

2-3 MARIQUITA IS CARVING HER WAY TO WINDWARD WITH A SINGLE REEF TUCKED IN. HERE SHE IS RACING IN A ROARING MISTRAL DURING THE 2006 VOILES DE ST. TROPEZ.

For a dose of reality, it might be worthwhile to go back in time and look at how our yachts were built. There is no doubt that most builders in that era of wood and steel (we shall ignore those rare forays into exotic materials like bronze and aluminum, which were almost invariably limited to specialized, single-purpose boats like America's Cup challengers and defenders) had access to excellent materials, skilled craftsmen and, generally speaking, state-of-the-art engineering. Indeed, we can fairly say that one of the reasons so many of those vintage yachts have been successfully restored is that they were so expertly constructed so that, even if neglected for a long period of time, they survived until an appreciative contemporary owner could restore them.

So many were, but not all, and not always. Then, as now, cost could be a deciding factor, especially with smaller yachts. While expertise cannot be dialed in at will – either the craftsmen have it or they don't – considerable savings can be achieved with different construction methods and by the use of less costly materials. In 1928 Gano Dunn, a respected American scientist and inventor, commissioned Goudy & Stevens of East Boothbay, Maine, to build him a 43-foot (13 m) schooner to a John G. Alden design. *Niliraga* "was built to a price", to use a characteristic Maine description. She had galvanized steel fastening and keel bolts, pine decks and iron ballast instead of the more expensive lead. She lasted over 40 years, but in the end there was nothing to restore and she was abandoned.

Even the great Herreshoff, although he would never compromise on engineering, would use cheaper materials if it meant selling boats. The New York Yacht Club 50s, for instance, were built using Herreshoff's diagonal hull strapping to stiffen the hulls. They soon developed problems with rust, as the straps were made of steel instead of the more expensive bronze.

The lesson learned from these examples is obvious: those lovely classics, whatever their vintage, design or construction, were not expected to last forever. The builders were aware of the limited life span of the wood and steel they used. Certainly in the case of racing boats, builders and owners were also aware of the constant evolution of design and technology, requiring that new boats be built to remain competitive. And that does not take into account evolving personal taste, changes in family status, the acquisition or loss of wealth and countless other factors that had little or nothing to do with dry rot, rust or maybe the adoption of a new rating rule. Thus it would be a mistake to attribute the demise or neglect of so many fine yachts simply to causes such as eventual material failure. Historically, yachts have been extensions of their owners' life, so the forces determining their fate are unavoidably more complex than simply a lifespan limited by corrosion or other structural limitations.

In addition the two World Wars caused a significant disruption in the sport of yachting as well as yacht building. While boat yards concentrated on military production, most amateur (and professional) sailors went to war, and the few who remained could not in good faith go sailing for the fun of it while their contemporaries were risking their lives. Military production meant anything from commissioning the Herreshoff Manufacturing Company to launch a series of patrol boats during World War I to, as was the case with the Henry R. Hinckley Company of Southwest Harbor, Maine, becoming

4-5 THE FIRST OF THE J-CLASS REPLICAS, RANGER, RACING IN THE 2010 MAXI ROLEX CUP OFF PORTO CERVO, SARDINIA. SHE WAS LAUNCHED IN 2004, THE FIRST J-CLASS YACHT TO BE BUILT IN MORE THAN 65 YEARS.

the nation's largest producer of life raft paddles in the Second World War.

The fact that the United States was remote from the actual fighting in most cases meant that yachts were simply laid up for the duration. Since the larger yachts used up substantial amounts of potentially strategic materials – there were a lot of bullets in a J-Class boat's keel – many of them were broken up during the late 1930s and early 1940s. But there probably were other forces at work as well, since the British Js and some members of the big boat class were put to rest in mud banks during World War II while England and Continental Europe were under attack and desperately needed raw materials for the war effort. Other than the royal yacht *Britannia*, the British Js survived. Indeed, other than *Endeavour II*, which was broken up as late as 1968, they have all been restored and are sailing today. None of the ten American J-Class sloops outlived World War II. While they surely contributed their raw materials to the military, very likely that contribution represented a relatively small proportion of the overall need.

In the 1930s the United States was in the grip of the Great Depression which, more than the war, may well have been the cause of the demise of those ten superb sailing yachts. In addition, Americans continued to view them as single-purpose machines meant almost exclusively for the America's Cup and thus disposable once they had served their purpose. Note that most other American yachts, great and small, did survive the war, although many that had been requisitioned by the Navy and Coast Guard as submarine patrol boats were usually returned to their owners in deplorably sad condition, with several put up for sale or abandoned as beyond repair and ultimately replaced.

Both wars saw yachting activities in Continental Europe severely curtailed, for obvious reasons. It is important to consider, too, that such disruptions delayed the recovery of the sport, as well as the resumption of building activities. For all their horror, wars usually bring about accelerated technological advances which often trickle down into less bellicose forms of "strife", if we may use that word for yacht racing. Such developments can often mean the forsaking of a formerly beloved craft in favor of a newer and perhaps faster or more competitive one.

Finally, the advent of molded fiberglass construction was arguably the principal factor in the dramatic change in yacht design and construction and in how sailors would think of their boats. While production yachts were nothing new – witness the plethora of one-design classes built in the early 20th century like S boats, Sound Interclubs, various versions of Dark Harbor knockabouts, Herreshoff 12s and their bigger sisters, the NYYC 40s and 50s, and later Owens cutters and many others – the fact is that GRP (glass-reinforced plastic) introduced a dramatic change in how boats were built and in how we perceived them. In a way, if the 1940s and '50s can be considered the end of the classic yacht era, it is because of this major shift in materials and mentality.

The effect of the introduction of the new material is relatively easy to understand: suddenly smaller to medium-size yachts could be endlessly reproduced on a scale heretofore unimaginable. In the face of increasing labor costs, GRP boats were more cost effective to build and less expensive to maintain. The loss of that indefinable property that made a boat a classic could be rationalized by the practical advantages, a rationalization made

6-7 *The J-Class sloop* Hanuman, *racing against* Ranger *at the Newport Bucket Regatta. She is a replica of the 1937 America's Cup challenger* Endeavour II *and the first modern J-Class replica to be built in aluminum under the new J-Class rules.*

easier by the fact that the early GRP production boats pretty much looked like their wooden counterparts, with long overhangs, graceful sheer and a proper yachtlike appearance.

The huge shift soon manifested itself in two principal ways. Yacht builders became, in many cases, boat factories intent on amortizing their tooling costs over the longest possible run of a given model. And on the racing front, rating rules changed, encouraging shapes which could not even charitably be considered graceful, never mind classic. The evolution of new shapes in turn led to the realization that GRP and its derivatives permitted hull forms that would have been unthinkable in wood.

This is a brief simplification of the transition from the era of individually crafted yachts to more streamlined and standardized production techniques. We must keep in mind that, through it all, custom boat building continued to endure, particularly in the case of larger yachts which naturally reflected their owners' individual tastes and requirements and were less subordinate to the need for economy.

When addressing the issue of how this transition of perception occurred, we have to consider the not insignificant role that subjectivity, prejudice and personal taste play in defining just what determines whether a particular boat meets the definition of a classic. Some are easy to identify: no one would dispute the classic status of a William Fife or Bjarne Aas design. Others are borderline and depend on intangibles like when she was built, her hull profile and other factors. It's a subject that has caused endless discussion in committees as the various governing bodies that control the proliferating classic yacht regattas and reunions around the world struggle with how to categorize the fleet – classics, new classics, restorations, rebuilds, in the spirit of tradition and so forth.

"I know one when I see one" – perhaps not such a bad definition after all.

Another of the truly fascinating aspects of a retrospective look at classic sailing yachts is to follow the development of boat building technology during that loosely circumscribed period which spanned the end of the 19th century until the moment when yachts ceased to be classics, a moment we can arbitrarily set at some point after World War II.

It is all too easy in this day of carbon fiber spars and hulls, aramid rigging, molded sails, in-boom furling systems and hydraulics everywhere to smile indulgently and speak of wooden ships and iron men when we see vintage gaff-rigged sloops or schooners sailing by. To give you an idea of the evolution in yachts over the past century, consider this: in 1903 *Reliance*, Herreshoff's mighty America's Cup defender, had a double steering wheel to allow two or three men to steer her in a breeze, and she raced with a crew of 64 hardy sailors. 100 years later, the 150-foot (45 m) ketch *Scheherazade*, designed by Bruce King and built at Hodgdon Yachts in East Boothbay, Maine, could be steered and trimmed by one person walking about the decks with a remote control.

But while we should admire the men who sailed those boats one hundred years ago, we should also take a close look at the unsuspected technological sophistication exhibited by the boats themselves. Some innovations were dead

8-9 *The lovely J-Class sloop Velsheda racing at the 2004 Maxi Rolex Cup off Porto Cervo, Sardinia. Velsheda was the only original J-Class yacht built in the 1930s that was not intended to compete in the America's Cup.*

ends, such as the combination of bronze bottom plating and aluminum topsides on the 1895 America's Cup cutter *Defender*. Given our current knowledge of galvanic action, we may once again smile indulgently at such apparent folly. But, absent that knowledge, the technological leap made sense. Another dead end was *Independence*, the freakish giant scow built for the 1901 Cup defense. In her case, the existing rating rule led her designers to outstrip the available structural technology – it was a case of "let's try it and let's hope." From launch to scrapping she lasted just about three months, during which time they could barely keep her afloat.

The same fertile brains that produced those two examples, however, were also at work inventing remarkably clever solutions to the many problems presented by the increasingly competitive atmosphere. By the time *Reliance* was launched, it was commonplace for those giant cutters to have take-up reels below decks to neatly stow sheet and halyard tails. But *Reliance* went one better: her mainsheet was made up of tapered rope. When on the wind, the six-part purchase on the boom used the heaviest segment of the sheet. Off the wind, when the load was greatly reduced, both ends were of gradually smaller diameter line and thus easier to handle and less likely to sag and drag in the water when running free – a small detail perhaps, but innovative nonetheless. In addition, her winches were so well designed and constructed that some continued to be used on a series of later America's Cup boats, including the 1937 *Ranger*.

It wasn't just on big boats that innovation mixed with tradition. In his constant quest for weight savings, Herreshoff developed his signature diagonal strapping system, which made for stiffer hulls while allowing somewhat thinner planking. He applied the technique to many of his smaller boats, such as the NYYC 40s and 50s.

But it was, as it always has been, the big racing boats that led the technological and innovative progression, because that's where the money was and that is where national prestige and the will to win at all costs drove designers and builders to seek new solutions. A 40-foot boat could sail and race effectively with a solid spruce mast, and if weight was really an issue that mast could be changed to a built-up hollow one. The big boats, however, were looking to remove tons of weight from their rigs, not mere hundreds of pounds. Hollow steel tube masts appeared at the end of the 19th century and became *de rigueur* after suitable trial and error, and note here that error usually meant a dismasting. The next logical step, as long as they were sailing with a hollow steel tube, was to design a topmast that would telescope inside it – a far more efficient and safer way to house it when necessary.

The advent of the Universal Rule, with its required adherence to Lloyd's A1 scantlings, made for racing boats of unprecedented structural strength. With the adoption of Marconi rigs, the added stiffness (the Seawanhaka Rule boats could barely hold up their extreme overhangs) of the hulls allowed greater rigging tension to the point that, when *Enterprise* showed up with her ugly riveted Duralumin mast in 1930, keeping those 160-foot (48 m) spars in column caused many anxious moments. This led to two contemporaneous solutions. First was a rule change dictating a great-

11 An aerial photo of the majestic gaff schooner Eleanora's bow, taken at the 2006 Voiles de St. Tropez. She is a recent replica of the famous racing schooner Westward.

17

ly increased minimum weight for masts, thus removing the temptation to build them excessively light and hence less safe. And second was the adoption of rod rigging, with its greater strength and reduced stretch. Sailors who raced in the 1970s will recall the endless debate about the safety of the new-fangled rod rigging then used on aluminum spars, a "new" technology that had been used, albeit it in a more limited fashion, 40 years previously.

During a sea trial on the new J-Class replica *Ranger*, Steve Wilson, then president of Southern Spars, was asked to compare her carbon fiber rig with the original boat's Duralumin spars. He gave the nod for pushing the envelope to the elder yacht: "The main issue was for us [Southern Spars] to design as light a rig as possible, but have it safe and stiff. The original Js were very aggressive from a design point of view as the materials they had ... were comparatively heavy to what we have now. Their rigs were quite 'on the edge' so they could be as light as possible." The original *Ranger's* mast, for instance, was built up of riveted aluminum plates of 20 different thicknesses to provide strength where needed and save weight where possible.

When leafing through old black-and-white photographs of pre-war yachts, note the set of their sails. It goes without saying that in, say, 1920 there were no CADCAMS, no molded sails, no Mylar or Kevlar or, for that matter, humble polyester. The only concession to modernity was the huge sewing machines used for seaming, with all else done by hand. But look at how well those sails flew – hardly a wrinkle, other than those induced by peaking, and gorgeous shape. You had to

know what you were doing with cotton sails and manila lines – gauge the humidity, and tension halyards and outhauls accordingly, lest you ruin the sails' shape as the cloth and rope shrank in a sudden fogbank. And there were tricks as well. Sailing downwind with sails trimmed in flat would shift the draft forward, a useful ruse just before the start of a race. In the first ten minutes to windward you enjoyed a speed bonus until the draft settled back. All those photos of yachts with loosely furled sails in their lazyjacks are not an indication of slovenly seamanship, either. You had to fight mildew constantly and keep your sails well aired out. In a way, this is one aspect of vintage sailing that today's restored classics and classic replicas have lost, since they all use synthetic sails.

A final instance of how those old classics were the result of perhaps more sophisticated thinking than we might now understand is in the use of the towing tank. Velocity prediction programs (VPP) have rendered this form of testing somewhat redundant, but back in 1900 George L. Watson was a pioneer, using the Denny test tank in Dumbarton, Scotland to try out his sailing yacht designs. It really wasn't until the 1937 America's Cup challenge that the towing tank once again played a crucial role, with Starling Burgess and Olin Stephens testing the six models for what was to become *Ranger* at the Stevens Institute of Technology in Hoboken, New Jersey. Today's tank testing, with highly sensitive load cells, telemetry and computer readouts, is a far cry from that era's methodology. Loads were measured by what were essentially spring scales, with mechanical analog readouts similar to old-fashioned butcher's scales, the data recorded by a technician running alongside the test model

12 MARIQUITA, SAILING DOWNWIND AT THE 2006 VOILES DE ST. TROPEZ WITH HER TRADITIONAL SINGLE-LUFF SPINNAKER. HER GRACEFUL SPREAD OF CANVAS TRULY EVOKES HER NICKNAME: THE LADYBIRD.

20-21 THE NEWLY LAUNCHED REPLICA OF RANGER MEETS THE RESTORED VELSHEDA AT THE 2004 ANTIGUA CLASSIC YACHT REGATTA. THE TWO J-CLASS SLOOPS SAILED THIS CLOSE TO EACH OTHER FOR THE ENTIRE REGATTA.

and then processed by slide rule. Sparkman & Stephens recently digitized all the original drawings for *Ranger* and developed VPP polars for all seven variants. While her original designers did indeed choose the best of the lot, the computer revealed that the "slowest" option was only giving away about three seconds per mile, a negligible and easily overcome divergence. The Sparkman & Stephens computer analysis revealed, among other things, how accurate the 1930s technology could be. In his memoirs (Olin J. Stephens II: *All This and Sailing, Too*, Mystic Seaport Museum, 1999) Olin Stephens remarked:

> "*Ranger has been incorrectly called a tank test product. Actually she was produced by her designers and selected by the tank. The tank was of inestimable value to us, for it told us what not to do, what not to build.*"

An indication of how determined Burgess and Stephens were to make sure they interpreted the towing tank results correctly is that they also built towing models to different scales to learn how to extrapolate the test numbers into meaningful full-scale specifications.

All of this highlights the fact that, for all the tradition and romance inextricably enmeshed in the history of classic yachts, they are actually illustrative of the evolution of the sport. This brief glimpse at some of the more esoteric, not to say less romantic, aspects of that history is intended to enhance our appreciation of these floating representatives of another era in yachting. Their grace and beauty is indisputable, and most of them are also infinitely rewarding to sail. A basic understanding of their perhaps less obvious background should only serve to deepen our appreciation.

And while a Dragon or a 25-foot gaff-rigged day sailer 80 years ago may not have had the benefit of as much of a technological approach to determine her lines and scantlings, it is still worth noting that their designers relied, quite likely, on more than just "an eye for fair lines."

Classic sailing yachts: for those of us who invariably turn our head whenever we spy one sailing by or at anchor, who indeed know one when we see one, there is nothing so gratifying as witnessing this remarkable renaissance of the genre. And we daresay that if William Fife or George L. Watson were to show up at, say, *Les Régates Royales* at Cannes, they probably would be pleasantly surprised at how many of their creations are still sailing (or sailing once again) and in excellent condition. We'll happily enjoy them all – restorations, replicas, modern derivations, all manifestations of sailors' appreciation of an aesthetic that has been kept alive and has gained new strength. The only sad part is that while we are fortunate that so many have survived, by design or happenstance, we really have no idea how many did not because they were broken up or abandoned, wrecked or sunk, though even those live on in spirit and give us pleasure through the imagination's eye and are nobly represented by their enduring sisters.

Perhaps in the end we simply need to faithfully discharge our role as caretakers of so much yachting history and not let shifts in the direction of the winds of fashion induce us to neglect our trusts. We can apply the sentiment expressed by Chummy Spurling shortly after his 100th birthday: "If I'd known I was going to live so long, I'd have taken better care of myself!"

22-23 *The Herreshoff gaff schooner* Mariette, *launched in 1915, charging to windward with all canvas set during the 2007 Antigua Classic Yacht Regatta.*

24-25 *A detailed photo of* Mariette's *foredeck crew in action during the 2006 Les Voiles de St. Tropez. Even though racing, she keeps her massive anchor catted and ready.*

THE SEAWANHAKA RULE YACHTS

VALKYRIE III

DEFENDER

SHAMROCK

COLUMBIA

SHAMROCK III

RELIANCE

Chapter *1*

They were huge, they were fast, they were outrageous and they were unbelievably beautiful. They sailed with crews of more than 50 men in those days of primitive or nonexistent winches, with one or two sailors up on the spreaders for an entire race. And they were boldly skippered by the likes of Hank Haff and Charlie Barr. Indeed, our great regret is that none of us were there to see them sail – it must have been a truly awesome sight

How outrageous were they? Just consider this: *Reliance*, the 1903 America's Cup defender, spread 16,000 square feet (1500 square m) of canvas on a 90-foot (27 m) waterline length. The 1937 defender, the J-Class *Ranger*, set a mere 7,545 square feet (697 square m) on an almost similar 87-foot (26 m) waterline. The latter's rig was all inboard, but *Reliance* measured over 200 feet (60 m) from the tip of her bowsprit to the end of the main boom.

The rating rule that spawned these extraordinary racing machines was the so-called Seawanhaka Rule, which measured waterline length and sail area, ignoring displacement, to arrive at a yacht's rating:

$$\frac{\text{Load Waterline Length} + \sqrt{\text{Sail Area}}}{2}$$

With no displacement factored in, designing a boat with the shortest possible waterline length for a given sail area was clearly the most advantageous solution. Since waterline length was measured with the boat upright, long overhangs dramatically increased the effective length when heeled over (and thus increased the boat's hull speed, or theoretical maximum speed) and, with the addition of a substantial bowsprit, provided an adequate platform to support the enormous rig.

The American boats derived an additional advantage from the way they were measured. Unlike the British challengers, they determined their flotation marks with no one aboard. A 50-man crew (*Reliance* sailed with 64), when shipped, could easily add 4 tons (3600 kg) of displacement, setting them down on their lines and giving them a bit of free unmeasured added waterline length and more than a little moveable ballast.

The fact that the rule ignored displacement inevitably led designers to make boats as light as possible, since a pound saved in the hull structure or rig was a crucial pound added to the lead ballast so necessary to keep those towering rigs standing up in a breeze.

When *Columbia* was launched in 1899, she had two masts: a steel mast with a telescoping wood topmast and, just in case, a wooden mast and topmast. She was measured for the wood spars, and as the steel mast was a full ton lighter, stepping it allowed her to ship additional lead ballast. In those days of empirical engineering, it should not have been a surprise that the steel rig collapsed during the first trial race.

The one memorable instance of weight-saving that failed spectacularly was, of course, *Defender*, the appropriately named 1895 Cup defender. While she used bronze plating for her bottom, as was common then, Herreshoff specified a new material, aluminum, for her topsides. Galvanic action was still an imprecisely understood principle at the time. Once launched into the salt water electrolyte, *Defender* barely made it through the America's Cup races without sinking.

They were the last of a breed, those great gaff-rigged sloops. The sailors who muscled them around the race course come hell or high tide became extinct with them, but while they sailed they must have been an exhilarating ride.

o wonder the British boats couldn't win the America's Cup – they had the wrong names! For the four Cup matches from 1895 to 1903 that witnessed the evolution of increasingly more extreme racing sloops, the American defenders continued the tradition of christening their yachts with sturdy, patriotic names: *Defender*, *Columbia*, *Reliance* and the defense contenders *Constitution* and *Independence*.

The challengers? Lord Dunraven, who was to fade away in disgrace after the '95 races, challenged with yachts bearing the warlike and dramatic, though not really representative, name *Valkyrie*. Sir Thomas Lipton was more whimsical and stayed true to his Irish roots with his challengers, all five of which were named *Shamrock*.

As one researches the early history of the America's Cup, from the late 19th century through the great days of the J Class in the 1930s, one of the recurring themes is the different philosophies behind big boat racing in the two countries. Basically, Americans viewed these monstrous contraptions as machines designed and built for the express purpose of defending the Cup. The British, meanwhile, cruised in their big boats and raced them every year. This dichotomy manifested itself in various ways, including how each side named its contenders.

Perhaps the proof of this theory lies in the fact that in 1930 the American *Enterprise* easily bested *Shamrock V*. There were four J's built for the defense: *Enterprise*, *Yankee*, *Weetamoe* and *Whirlwind*. Guess which two were the finalists? Finally, in 1934 and 1937 the British mounted serious challenges with J-Class yachts bearing the more purposeful name *Endeavour*. Indeed, in 1934 *Endeavour* almost beat the defender, the poetically named *Rainbow* – another indication that names do matter. The Americans learned their lesson; in 1937 they defended the Cup with *Ranger*.

But back in 1895 the issue of performance as re-

lated to yacht name was still in its initial stages. The real debate was about beam and draft, with the British initially adhering to their traditional narrow, deep cutter configuration while the Americans favored beamy, shallower draft yachts. The Seawanhaka Rule forced both sides to reconsider. Once the challenger and the New York Yacht Club agreed on the waterline length, a boat's sail area essentially determined her rating. As in any class of racing yachts built to a rule, designs first tended to differ noticeably before empirical observation eventually resulted in increasingly similar boats.

Both sides were sufficiently open-minded to learn from each other. For the '95 Cup, Lord Dunraven's *Valkyrie III* was uncharacteristically beamy, more so than the American *Defender*. While no one would claim that a yacht's design was no longer a relevant issue, the convergence of design philosophies meant that technology, in the form of materials and mechanical contrivances, played an increasingly important role, not to mention the skipper and the crew.

A good example of how technology played an essential role in the 1895 America's Cup can be seen from the construction of the two boats involved. *Valkyrie III* was designed by George L. Watson, the famed Scottish naval architect. She was built of composite construction with elm and teak planking on steel frames, which was a typical construction technique for large yachts in those days. Her dimensions were almost identical to the defender's. The most striking difference between the two boats was that Nathanael Herreshoff, *Defender*'s designer and builder, was far more daring in his engineering solution to hull structure: she was built of manganese bronze bottom plating and aluminum topsides over steel frames.

This novel construction method had two results. In theory it made for a strong, rigid and above all lightweight hull, which meant the weight savings could be added to the lead ballast, thus creating

28-29 Defender (left) and Valkyrie III (right) jockeying for position before the start of the September 7, 1895, America's Cup Race. Note the topman sitting on Valkyrie III's jumper strut. The 1895 Cup challenge was marred by ill feeling on both sides.

28

a stiffer boat able to carry a greater press of canvas. But it also created what was essentially a floating battery. The folly of combining three dissimilar metals in a salt water environment may be obvious with the scientific knowledge gained over 100 years later, but at the time, with no awareness of the principle of electrolysis, it was considered a brilliant stroke. And considering that *Defender* managed to keep bottom and topsides together at least for the duration of the Cup campaign, the concept could be considered successful. There were reports of structural problems as that Cup season unfolded. If true, it would hardly be surprising since the galvanic gremlins lost no time in making their presence felt.

Defender was also well sailed by a hardy crew of Maine fishermen. Herbert Stone and William Taylor, in their book *The America's Cup Races* (New York, Van Nostrand, 1958) relate how her skipper, the renowned Hank Haff, "picked up a crew from Deer Island ... but they were a good crew and under old 'Hank' they made the 'brass' boat go." Patriotic feelings ran high, and a native crew was deemed more appropriate than the usual "squarehead" Norwegian sailors previously engaged.

The more conventional *Valkyrie III* reported no structural problems after the Cup races, although she did need repairs after her passage across the Atlantic, an indication of how lightly built these boats were in those unregulated days and of the handicap imposed on the challengers, which had to sail to the match "on their own bottom," as the Cup Deed of Gift required. But she lost the match, both on the water to the faster *Defender* and in the Committee room when disqualified for fouling her competitor. Lord Dunraven accused the Americans of cheating – a matter of a misunderstanding over *Defender*'s shifting internal ballast – and departed after the New York Yacht Club revoked his honorary membership.

30-31 DEFENDER, THE APPROPRIATELY NAMED 1895 AMERICA'S CUP DEFENDER, STILL PRESUMABLY UNAFFECTED BY THE GALVANIC CORROSION OF HER HULL PLATING. THE PHOTO SHOWS THE LATERAL STAYS NEEDED TO KEEP HER MASSIVE BOOM FROM BENDING EXCESSIVELY.

31 VALKYRIE III, IN A PHOTOGRAPH TAKEN ON SEPTEMBER 10, 1895. SHE LOST HER CHALLENGE FOR THE AMERICA'S CUP, BUT AT LEAST HER COMPOSITE CONSTRUCTION KEPT HER SEAWORTHY, UNLIKE THE WINNER, DEFENDER.

32 SIR THOMAS LIPTON'S FIRST CHALLENGER, SHAMROCK, SAILING WITH HER SPINNAKER POLE SET DURING THE 1899 AMERICA'S CUP. TAKING AN ACTION PHOTO FROM THE END OF THE BOWSPRIT WITH A WOODEN BOX CAMERA AND GLASS PLATES WAS NO MEAN CHALLENGE!

33 COLUMBIA, THE 1899 DEFENDER, SAILING TO WINDWARD WITH ALL CANVAS DRAWING PERFECTLY. THE CALM SEA IS AN INDICATION OF HOW POWERFUL THE SEAWANHAKA RULE YACHTS WERE: SHE'S RAIL DOWN IN WHAT WOULD SEEM TO BE AT BEST AN EIGHT-KNOT BREEZE.

Evidently, *Defender's* galvanic woes remained a well-guarded secret. For the 1899 America's Cup challenge, William Fife decided to borrow a page out of Herreshoff's notebook and specified bronze bottom plating and aluminum topsides for *Shamrock*, the new sloop built for Sir Thomas Lipton. J. Thorneycroft & Co., her builder, had considerable experience building lightweight patrol boats. Perhaps this fact (or the habit of maintaining secrecy instilled by their military clients) explains why there were no reports of mysterious corrosive action.

In keeping with the principle of cross pollination, it was the Americans' turn to take a more conservative approach. *Columbia,* the Herreshoff-designed and built defender, was constructed of Tobin bronze plates over nickel steel frames, an expensive but electrolytically-inactive solution. She was rigged with a traditional Oregon pine mast, although Herreshoff also built a steel spar for her that was eventually stepped to form an innovative rig with a telescoping wooden topmast. Nathanael's brother, the almost

blind J.B. Herreshoff, reputedly tapped the steel mast with his walking stick and predicted that it would never work. It collapsed during the first trial race against the rebuilt *Defender,* which sailed as a trial horse.

Meanwhile, *Shamrock* was having her own problems with her steel mast. It was too bendy, which, besides threatening to collapse, made it impossible to maintain sail shape. Empirical engineering was clearly in evidence, as this was the first time steel spars had been used in these enormous sloops. Both designers were clearly on the steep upward slope of the learning curve.

Not surprisingly, the convergence of design philosophies produced two very evenly matched boats. *Columbia* won all three races but by unprecedented narrow margins: one minute and 20 seconds, three minutes and 45 seconds, and 41 seconds. Charlie Barr, her professional skipper, was believed to have made the difference between victory and defeat.

Columbia came back to defend the Cup again in 1901, beating out the new *Constitution* and the giant scow *Independence*, which could be blindingly fast in certain conditions but mostly suffered structural problems and was unreliable – so unreliable, in fact, that she was scrapped before the Cup races even began.

The innovation from that year's match came from G.L. Watson, who for the first time in sailing history subjected his design for *Shamrock II* to extensive tank testing. Tank testing sailing yachts was still an inexact science as the forces acting on the boat could not be accurately quantified, but Watson was 36 years ahead of Starling Burgess and Olin Stephens, the designers of *Ranger*, who were the next America's Cup designers to rely on the towing tank. *Columbia* beat *Shamrock II* convincingly, and Watson was heard to remark that he wished that Herreshoff had used a test tank to beat him instead of relying on his eye for lines. Herbert Stone and William Taylor summed up the match with a bold prediction:

> "After the Cup Race of 1901 it began to be apparent ... that the limit to which everything could be sacrificed for speed in racing yachts had been reached."

34-35 Shamrock II and Columbia *circling just before the start of the October 1, 1901, America's Cup race. Shamrock II's knuckle bow was a feature which later appeared in many of G. L. Watson's designs.*

36 THE 1903 AMERICA'S CUP CHALLENGER, SIR THOMAS LIPTON'S SHAMROCK III. AS HAD BECOME COMMON PRACTICE STARTING WITH COLUMBIA, SHE WAS RIGGED WITH A HOLLOW STEEL MAST AND A WOODEN TOPMAST WHICH COULD BE HOUSED BY TELESCOPING INTO THE BOTTOM SECTION.

37 SIR THOMAS LIPTON IN A RARE PHOTO SHOWING HIM ACTUALLY SAILING. WHILE PASSIONATE ABOUT BEAUTIFUL SAILING YACHTS (HE OWNED A 23-METRE CUTTER NAMED SHAMROCK AS WELL AS HIS VARIOUS AMERICA'S CUP CHALLENGERS) HE ALMOST INVARIABLY PREFERRED TO OBSERVE THE RACES FROM HIS STEAM YACHT.

Those were prophetic words, but prophecies did not always apply to Nathanael Herreshoff. With *Reliance*, the defender for the 1903 America's Cup, he pulled out all the stops and created his masterpiece, the culmination of accumulated experience in racing yacht design. She was breath takingly powerful, majestic to behold and changed the racing scene forever.

Sir Thomas Lipton turned to William Fife for his challenger, and *Shamrock III* was to be the last America's Cup boat Fife designed. There is no record of any tank testing of his design, even though she was built at William Denny and Brothers shipyard, where the towing tank previously used by G.L. Watson was located. If Fife is remembered for anything, it is his uncanny eye in drawing a boat's lines. Every yacht that came from his drawing board was a lovely creation of perfect proportions and harmony. *Shamrock III* was no exception, combining

speed and beauty and with neither quality compromised.

She was conservatively built of nickel steel coated with enamel and she had a pine deck. Her rig followed what had by then become standard practice for these big sloops – she had a steel mast with wooden topmast. She departed from standard British practice by having a steering wheel instead of the usual massive tiller controlled by relieving tackles.

But 1903 was not the year to be conservative. Herreshoff had observed the brief, unhappy career of the ill-fated *Independence* in 1901 and successfully incorporated her positive features – extreme overhangs, flat bottom and vast sail area – into *Reliance* while also giving *Reliance's* steel hull adequate structural integrity. Admittedly, she did have some structural problems with her long ends, but she lasted the season and her sailing prowess

38 *The 1903 Cup defender Reliance in Drydock is a breathtaking example of how extreme the America's Cup yachts had become. While her lines were undoubtedly beautiful, she implausibly set 16,000 square feet (1500 sq m) of canvas on her 90-foot (27 m) waterline.*

38-39 *Reliance, here seen sailing in light air, was the glorious swan song of the Seawanhaka Rule yachts.*

made everyone forget her issues. Consider, for a moment, those overhangs: over 50 feet (15 m) added to her 90-foot (27 m) waterline, which meant that when she heeled over her effective waterline length increased by more than 40 percent. That figure pretty much says it all – she was unbeatable and won all three Cup races. True, the third win was due in part to *Shamrock III* getting lost in the fog, but *Reliance* was ahead anyway.

One adjective which needs to be added to *Reliance*'s lexicon of superlatives is "very scary." While

she was the result of the single-minded pursuit of speed under sail, she was also a dead end. This was demonstrated by *Independence*, which in many ways had been more extreme than *Reliance*. Perhaps *Reliance*'s ultimate contribution was that she made the defenders and challengers for the America's Cup inject a dose of sanity – and good seamanship – into the contest and close the chapter on these amazing over-canvassed craft. The New York Yacht Club adopted the Universal Rule, Lloyd's scantlings and all, and big boat racing remained just as thrilling as ever.

THE CLASSICS

Chapter 2

We thought that choosing a few representative yachts to include in this chapter would be somewhat like holding an audition – scroll down a list of likely candidates and simply choose a few that stand out as being either more interesting or more famous and they would obviously be good selections. The fact is, classic yachts are not that easy to categorize. And despite the many *Concours d'Elegances* that have become fashionable at classic yacht events, it is not possible to assign them a rank.

Anyone who has walked along the dock at Les Régates Royales or perhaps the Antigua Classic Yacht Regatta can tell you that every single boat there has something of interest to hold your attention. It could be a cherished, family-owned and personally-maintained 30-foot (9 m) gaff cutter, her varnish perhaps in need of a touch-up and with a couple of rope ends in need of a fresh whipping. Or it might be a professionally-restored and sailed 90-foot (27 m) ketch with perfectly polished brass and not an Irish pennant in sight. Either one is a priceless and treasured craft, well deserving of being included.

Furthermore, it makes sense to include some boats that no longer exist in order to offer as complete a picture as possible and give a balanced and comprehensive overview of classic yachting. After all, the mere fact that no one ever restored a particular boat because she was sent to the ship breakers so her owner could use her valuable gear for another boat or perhaps because she simply disappeared does not diminish her importance in any way. Classic yachts have a way of staying alive through faded sepia photos, old memories and names engraved on sterling silver trophies.

Several of the yachts were raced when new,

and some were enjoyed for cruising. Most, not surprisingly, saw a bit of both activities. With the proliferation of classic yacht regattas, it may seem that all restored classics are raced these days, but that would be misconstruing what the regattas are really all about. To be sure, there is competition, often keen and antagonistic. After all, why undertake the expense and effort to restore or replicate a classic yacht famous for her racing prowess if not to take her racing again, especially now that there are so many tempting opportunities? But look carefully at the assembled multitude of vessels at any one of these events and, nestled among Fife's and Herreshoff's and Stephens's vintage racing creations, you will find beloved old wooden craft which are there just for the shared joy of it all. They will sail out in the morning, eventually cross the starting line, then typically continue haphazardly until lunch or a cooling swim becomes more important.

As we said, they're all deserving of our consideration. By keeping our eyes and mind open, we come to appreciate the truly astounding variety of yachts, great and small, built before boat yards became factories. Before new materials allowed the infinite replication of a single design, each boat, no matter how humble, was *sui generis* – a unique expression of her builder's craft.

In this chapter, it may seem as if we have devoted the lion's share of space to William Fife's yachts. The other designers represented, to be sure, were no less talented and produced worthy rivals to Fife's creations. Many years ago, the host of a classical (that word "classic" crops up in so many contexts) music program was asked why he played so much Mozart. His reply was, "Why, there is no such thing as too much Mozart!" So in keeping with that spirit, it is impossible to feature too many of Fife's yachts.

METEOR III and BRITANNIA

THE IMPERIAL YACHTS

METEOR III

TYPE: gaff topsail schooner
LOA: 161 ft (49 m)
BEAM: 27 ft (8.2 m)
DRAFT: 16 ft (4.8 m)
HULL MATERIAL: steel
DESIGNER: H. G. Barbey & A. Cary Smith
BUILDER: Townsend & Downey Shipbuilding, New Jersey, USA
YEAR BUILT: 1902

We all owe a great debt to "Tum-Tum". King Edward VII's notorious appetite for life included sailing, and in 1893 he commissioned G.L. Watson to design the royal yacht *Britannia*, whose racing record remains unparalleled. He was still Prince of Wales at the time (his nickname a reflection of his girth) and did not ascend to the British throne until 1902. He died in 1910, succeeded by George V, who continued racing and winning until both he and his lovely yacht were buried in 1936.

The debt we owe both monarchs is that over her long life *Britannia* was constantly kept up to date to remain competitive in the big boat races that were so popular then. She was re-rigged no less than seven times – the first five were variations on the gaff cutter rig, the final two as a Marconi sloop to rate in the J Class. You can trace the evolution in design theory (and practice) as her gaff cutter rig became narrower and taller over time until the change to J rating in 1931 and the final modification, Park Avenue boom and all, in 1935. She remained competitive almost until the end, although more evolved boats like *Endeavour* eventually outclassed her.

While *Britannia* was instrumental in keeping the big boat class alive, racing against His Majesty must have been somewhat unnerving. In his book *Enterprise to Endeavour* (Adlard Coles Nautical, London, 1999) Ian Dear points out that only the schooner *Westward* dared force *Britannia* to tack; all others would steer around her. One wonders how this might have affected her singularly successful racing career. She celebrated her 200th win at the 1930 Cowes Week. King George V, despite publicity photographs showing him at the wheel or pulling on a line, never steered while racing, instead letting his professional crew sail the boat. His Majesty did love her, however, and asked that she be buried at sea when he died. In 1936, shortly after he passed on, *Britannia* was stripped of her spars and gear, towed out and sunk by gunfire from a Navy ship.

One of her close competitors for a brief period of time in the early 1900s was another royal (actually, in this case, imperial) yacht: *Meteor III*. Kaiser Wilhelm II – who was, among his tangled lineage, Queen Victoria's grandchild and thus Tum-Tum's nephew – was impressed with Nathanael Herreshoff's schooner *Ingomar* when he saw her racing in England. He contacted Herreshoff about building a similar yacht, but when he tried to dictate (he was, after all, an emperor) some design changes, the Wizard of Bristol suggested he look for another builder.

In the end, *Meteor III* was designed by A. Cary Smith and built at the Downey Shipbuilding Company on Shooters Island in Newark Bay. She was christened by Alice Roosevelt. Unlike his English relatives, Wilhelm II was an able yachtsman and would steer his schooner when racing. And unlike *Britannia*, which was used primarily for day racing, *Meteor III* was luxuriously appointed below decks.

Meteor III raced in England and Germany after her launch before being sold in 1908. She changed owners several times, eventually cruising in the Pacific for several years. She ended her days sadly, sold to a ship breaker in Staten Island, in sight of her birthplace on Shooters Island.

BRITANNIA

TYPE: "Big Class" gaff cutter changed to Marconi sloop
LOA: 122 ft (37.1 m)
BEAM: 24 ft (7.3 m)
DRAFT: 15 ft (4.6 m)
SAIL AREA: 10,324 sq ft (960 sq m)
HULL MATERIAL: steel
BUILDER: D&W Henderson Shipyard Ltd, UK
YEAR BUILT: 1893

42 KAISER WILHELM II'S SCHOONER METEOR III, SAILING OFF HELGOLAND IN 1908. SHE WAS DE-SIGNED AND BUILT IN THE UNITED STATES, ALTHOUGH HERRESHOFF REFUSED THE COMMISSION AFTER THE KAISER DARED TO MAKE SOME SUGGESTIONS REGARDING HER DESIGN.

44-45 KING GEORGE V AT THE HELM OF THE ROYAL YACHT BRITANNIA, IN A WELL-ORCHESTRATED PUB-LICITY PHOTO. UNLIKE HIS COUSIN, KAISER WILHELM II, WHO WAS AN EXCELLENT SAILOR, THE KING RARELY SAILED ON BRITANNIA AND ALMOST NEVER TOUCHED THE HELM. HE WAS NONETHELESS PASSION-ATE ABOUT HER.

45 THE CREW OF THE ROYAL YACHT BRITANNIA HOISTING HER MAINSAIL. THE TWO GANGS OF SAILORS ARE HEAVING ON THE PEAK AND THROAT HALYARDS SIMULTANEOUSLY, WITH NO WINCHES IN SIGHT.

46 *The Royal Yacht Britannia reaching along on port tack. She is flying an unusual ballooner staysail, presumably effective in those conditions.*

47 *King George V (wearing a sailor's round hat) lending a hand trimming a sheet on board Britannia during a regatta at Cowes, in August, 1921. This is almost surely another posed photograph to enhance His Majesty's image as a sailor.*

PEN DUICK

TYPE: gaff-rigged cutter
LOA: 50 ft (15.1 m)
LWL: 32 ft (10 m)
BEAM: 10 ft (2.9 m)
DRAFT: 7 ft (2.2 m)
SAIL AREA: 1,720 sq ft (160 sq m)
HULL MATERIAL: wood, later fiberglassed
DESIGNER: William Fife III
BUILDER: Gridiron and Workers Shipyard, Ireland
YEAR BUILT: 1898
YEAR RESTORED: 1958/1989

*S*he started more than 110 years ago as *Yum*, a 32-foot (10 m) waterline gaff cutter from the drawing board of William Fife. Unlike so many of Fife's creations, she was not built at his Fairlie yard but at the Gridiron and Workers shipyard in Crosshaven, Ireland. Her first owner was Adolphus Fowler, a member of the Royal Cork Yacht Club. Fowler only kept her for four years, after which she changed names no less than seven times before, in 1938, being christened *Pen Duick* (Breton dialect for "coal tit bird"), the name made famous by her owner, the eminent French sailor Eric Tabarly.

Tabarly became *Pen Duick*'s fifteenth owner when he bought her from his father in 1952. Throughout a remarkable sailing career which included several much more modern and experimental (*Pen Duick VI* used spent uranium as ballast) yachts – all named *Pen Duick* – he never lost his attachment for his lovely little cutter and continued sailing her whenever he could.

By 1958 *Pen Duick* was showing her age. She was consigned to the Constantini yard in La Trinité for what was to be a pragmatic, if perhaps not truly authentic, refit. Tabarly had limited resources and limited time to sail her, and he realized that his best option would be to concentrate on making her seaworthy and safe; for instance, he covered her hull with fiberglass. Purists may shudder at the idea, but there is a great deal to be said for pro-

longing a classic yacht's life and extending the pleasure she can give to those who sail her. Needless to say, not all sailors or owners of older boats can devote the financial resources necessary for a restoration using traditional techniques and materials. GRP, at the time a relatively new material, offered an affordable means for holding on to one's cherished old boat.

Pen Duick continued to be somewhat neglected by Tabarly, whose sailing schedule kept him at sea much of the time, and by 1983 she showed clear signs of needing more attention. She was towed to the Raymond Labbé yard in St. Malo and once again underwent a gradual refit. By 1989 she was back afloat, joining the growing fleet of classic yachts that raced in the newly formed regatta circuit. In May of 1998 Tabarly held a 100th anniversary celebration for her. A week later he decided to sail to Scotland for a memorial regatta in honor of her creator, William Fife.

Tabarly had always been a traditional, if not old fashioned, sailor. He believed in the maxim "one hand for the ship and one hand for yourself" and steadfastly avoided life jackets and safety harnesses. During the night of June 12 the Irish Sea claimed him. He had gone forward to hand a headsail and was swept overboard. *Pen Duick* survives him, still owned and cherished by the Tabarly family, an enduring memorial to a great sailor.

48-49 Marie Tabarly sailing Pen Duick off Brest in a two-reef breeze. Like many similar century-old classics, constant restorations enable her to be enjoyed in challenging sailing conditions.

50-51 The late Eric Tabarly swaying up a jib halyard on Pen Duick. The photo was taken shortly before Tabarly was lost at sea. Unlike many restored classic yachts, which gleam with polished bronze and flawless varnish, he kept Pen Duick practical, as evidenced by the galvanized steel fittings.

52 AND 53 *TWO AERIAL PHOTOS OF* PEN DUICK, *TAKEN BEFORE AND AFTER SHE HAS SET HER FORESTAY-SAIL, FLYING JIB AND CLUB TOPSAIL.*

54 *Classic yacht racing on board* Pen Duick. *The majestic gaff schooner* Eleanora *is sailing off her starboard quarter with all light canvas set.*

55 Pen Duick *sailing during her 100th anniversary commemoration on May 31, 1998. The late Eric Tabarly organized the event to celebrate her latest refit and the fact that she was once again seaworthy.*

MOONBEAM III

TYPE: cutter
LOA: 102 ft (31 m) w/ bowsprit
LOD: 81 ft (24.7 m)
LWL: 62 ft (19 m)
BEAM: 15.5 ft (4.7 m)
DRAFT: 12 ft (3.6 m)
SAIL AREA: 4,630 sq ft (430 sq m)
HULL MATERIAL: teak/elm/oak frames
DESIGNER: William Fife III
BUILDER: William Fife & Son/rebuilt: Monaco Marine
YEAR BUILT: 1903
YEAR RESTORED: 2006

She was launched at William Fife's Fairlie yard in 1903 and christened *Moonbeam III* – the third of a series of four *Moonbeams* that Fife designed and built for Charles Plumtree Johnson starting in 1864; the fourth and last one launched in 1920, just after the end of World War I.

Fife's design No. 491, *Moonbeam III*, was typical of his gaff-rigged racing cutters of that period, with flush decks, tiller steering and huge sail plans. Construction was quite typical as well, with teak and elm planking on oak frames. Johnson raced her actively in the decade before the war and sold her in 1920 when he took delivery of his new boat. *Moonbeam III* acquired a gasoline engine in 1924 and then changed ownership several times in the following years.

Following a familiar pattern for so many classic yachts of the early 20th century, she entered a period of relative neglect, occasionally sailing and racing out of Cannes, France. She was then sold to Félix Amiot, a French aviation pioneer who also owned a shipyard near Cherbourg in Normandy. Amiot laid her up for 24 years, from 1947 until 1971, at which time she was sold. She then spent several years sailing in the Aegean. In 1979, *Moonbeam III* was loaded on a cargo ship and sent to the Camper & Nicholson shipyard in the UK, where she was once again laid up, this time for 10 years. While at Nicholson's, she was fitted with a steering wheel and some winches and electronic navigation gear.

Moonbeam III was sold at auction by Sotheby's in 1989, then changed owners a few more times until she was brought to St. Tropez where, in 2001, she finally found the owner she deserved – Didier Waechter, an avid sailor and lover of classic yachts who also owned the Camper & Nicholson 1904 classic *Merrymaid*. Waechter died in 2004, shortly after acquiring the renamed *Moonbeam of Fife*. Upon inheriting the yacht, his daughter, inspired by a visit onboard *Mariquita*, which had just been restored by Fairlie Restorations, decided to keep her and start a thorough refit. The first phase was a structural overhaul at Monaco Marine shipyard, near the Marines de Cogolin. Among other problems, a more than 1 inch (2.5 cm) gap was found between the ribs and keel, highlighting the timeliness of the work. She was launched for the 2005 sailing season before being sent to Fairlie Restorations for the second phase, which involved the total restoration of her mahogany and leather interior, complete in every period detail.

After a hundred years of frequent changes of ownership and long periods of inactivity, *Moonbeam of Fife* has settled into her well-deserved second life.

56-57 MOONBEAM III (NOW KNOWN AS MOONBEAM OF FIFE) WITH HER ORIGINAL — AND SHORT-LIVED — GAFF YAWL RIG. SHE WAS CON-VERTED TO HER GAFF CUTTER RIG TO MAKE HER A COMPETITIVE RACER. NOTE THE GRACEFUL CURVED BOOMKIN FOR THE MIZZEN SHEET.

58-59 MOONBEAM III SHOWING OFF HER RACING TRIM DURING A CLASSIC YACHT REGATTA. THE CREW SPORTS APPROPRIATE WHITE UNI-FORMS, IN KEEPING WITH THE YACHT'S TRADITIONAL CHARACTER. HER SAILS ARE FROM THE RATSEY & LAPTHORN LOFT, WHICH PROBABLY CUT HER ORIGINAL SUIT MORE THAN A HUNDRED YEARS AGO.

60-61 FAIRLIE RESTORATIONS WERE COMMISSIONED TO RESTORE MOONBEAM III'S INTERIOR. THE TUFTED LEATHER SETTEES AND VARNISHED RAISED PANELS RECAPTURE THE PERIOD ATMOSPHERE PERFECTLY. LEFT, THE MAIN SALOON, WITH THE EXPOSED DECK BEAMS TYPICAL OF THE ERA. ABOVE, A GUEST STATEROOM.

62-63 MOONBEAM III BOWLING ALONG ON A BEAM REACH IN THE GULF OF ST. TROPEZ DURING THE FINAL REGATTA IN THE CLASSIC YACHT
CIRCUIT: LES VOILES DE ST. TROPEZ.

MARIQUITA

TYPE: 19-Metre gaff cutter
LOA: 125 ft (38.1 m)
LWL: 66 ft (20.1 m)
BEAM: 17 ft (5.2 m)
DRAFT: 11.5 ft (3.5 m)
SAIL AREA: 6,260 sq ft (582 sq m)
HULL MATERIAL: steel framed/wooden/teak
DESIGNER: William Fife III
BUILDER: William Fife & Son, Scotland
YEAR BUILT: 1911
YEAR RESTORED: 2004

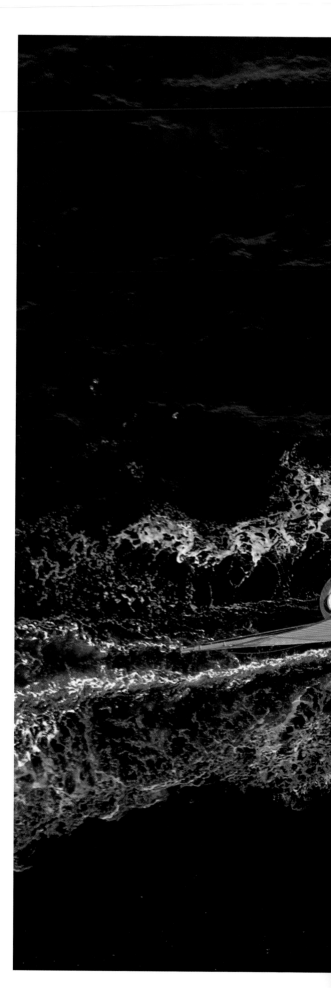

There is an old sepia tone photograph signed by the famous yachting photographer Beken of Cowes and bearing a legend in white ink: "*Mariquita, 1912.*" If we could just reproduce that photo, there would be no need to write one more word about *Mariquita*. She is on a beam reach flying a huge club topsail, every bit of canvas set just so, a bone in her teeth and the quarter wave cresting at her taffrail. We can easily transpose ourselves on board and share the exhilaration of her crew, witness her skipper's apprehensive occasional glance aloft and appreciate the happy synthesis of beauty, speed and elation.

Mariquita, "the ladybird", was built in 1911, so this photo was taken during her second racing season. She was not a "classic" then but a state-of-the-art racing machine, built to the International 19-Meter Rule. Her beauty and speed can be summed up succinctly in one word: Fife. She was designed by the great William Fife and built at his yard in Fairlie, Scotland.

The first International Rule made provision for three classes of big boats: 12 Metres, 15 Metres and the majestic 23-Metres, which are very similar to the J Class in size. A group of British yachtsmen who felt that the 23-Metre yachts were too expensive while the 15 Metre class was not quite large enough for regattas in continental Europe commissioned four cutters rating 62 feet (19 m) for the 1911 racing season. One of those men, A.K. Stothert, was *Mariquita's* owner.

The ladybird had a successful first season of rac-

ing, helped in no small part by Sir Thomas Lipton's loan of a skipper, the famous Captain Sycamore, and crucial crew members from his 23-Metre *Shamrock* (not to be confused with his J-Class *Shamrock*); Sir Thomas, while not a sailor himself, simply enjoyed owning beautiful yachts. In 1912 the 19-Metre foursome sailed to Kiel in Germany, in addition to continuing their racing in English waters. By 1913 the class was already waning, with only two boats sailing.

At the outbreak of World War I, *Mariquita* was sold to a Norwegian and renamed *Maud IV*. She was bought back into British ownership after the war, but the 19 Metres never raced again as a class. She was sold again in 1924, her sail area was reduced and she was used as a cruising yacht, occasionally racing in handicap classes. Her owner, Alan Messer, cruised to the Baltic several times. With another world war looming, she was sold off as a houseboat at Pin Mill, Suffolk, with her mast cut off and her lead ballast removed.

It was not until 1991 that she was rescued and brought to the appropriately named Fairlie Restorations, Ltd., where, beginning in 2001, she was given a complete structural and cosmetic rebuild. Since 2004, *Mariquita* has been competing in vintage yacht events against many of her Fife siblings and is a much admired and much photographed classic. Although, as lovely as she is now when captured on color film, there is something about that sepia photograph ... some impressions you simply can't restore.

64-65 THE GAFF CUTTER MARIQUITA, SAILING INTO THE GULF OF ST. TROPEZ IN OCTOBER 2006 TO COMPETE IN THAT YEAR'S LES VOILES DE ST. TROPEZ. THE AERIAL PHOTO SHOWS HOW WEATHERLY THE NEARLY 100-YEAR-OLD YACHT COULD STILL BE.

66-67 WILLIAM FIFE MEETS NATHANAEL HERRESHOFF: THE GAFF SCHOONER MARIETTE, ON STARBOARD TACK, IS ABOUT TO CROSS MARIQUITA'S BOW. THE DETAILS SHOWN IN THIS PHOTOGRAPH DEPICT HOW LOVINGLY AND EXPERTLY MARIQUITA HAS BEEN RESTORED.

68 AND 68-69 FAIRLIE RESTORATIONS WAS RESPONSIBLE FOR THE SUPERBLY EXECUTED RESTORATION OF MARIQUITA'S INTERIOR ACCOMMODATIONS. SHOWN HERE IS HER MAIN SALOON, LOOKING FORWARD TO THE GALLEY AND CREW QUARTERS.

70 ANOTHER AERIAL PHOTO-GRAPH OF MARIQUITA, THE "LADYBIRD," WITH A BONE IN HER TEETH AS SHE SAILS TO WINDWARD. NOTE THE SPIN-NAKER POLE STOWED VERTICAL-LY AGAINST THE MAST. SHE AL-SO DISPLAYS THE TRADITIONAL VARNISHED DINGHY LASHED DOWN ON DECK.

71 NOT A JOB FOR THE FAINT OF HEART: THE TOPMAN ON MARIQUITA STANDING ON THE JUMPER STRUT DURING A TACK. HIS PRINCIPAL JOB IS TO ASSIST IN SETTING AND TACKING THE CLUB TOPSAIL. HE ALSO KEEPS AN EYE ON THE INTRICATE RUN-NING RIGGING.

72-73 MARIQUITA CLOSE HAULED ON STARBOARD TACK DURING
LES RÉGATES ROYALES AT CANNES IN 2005. IT IS A TRIBUTE TO THE
QUALITY OF THE RESTORATION CREWS, AS WELL AS TO THE ENTHUSI-
ASM OF HER SAILORS, THAT SHE IS BEING DRIVEN SO HARD.

SUMURUN

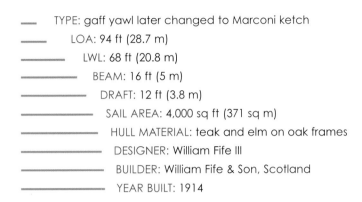

TYPE: gaff yawl later changed to Marconi ketch
LOA: 94 ft (28.7 m)
LWL: 68 ft (20.8 m)
BEAM: 16 ft (5 m)
DRAFT: 12 ft (3.8 m)
SAIL AREA: 4,000 sq ft (371 sq m)
HULL MATERIAL: teak and elm on oak frames
DESIGNER: William Fife III
BUILDER: William Fife & Son, Scotland
YEAR BUILT: 1914

There is nothing like the whiff of scandal to add spice to a story, although *Sumurun's* story certainly does not need any embellishment. She is old enough, known well enough and certainly beautiful enough to hold her own. She was designed and built by William Fife in 1914 at Fairlie, Scotland. Originally rigged as a gaff yawl, she did not really start her career until 1920 because World War I broke out shortly after her launch.

Although designed for luxurious cruising, *Sumurun* originally was not fitted with auxiliary power, relying instead on her motor tender to tow her in and out of harbors. Interestingly, however, she was equipped with a generator to power her electric lights. Another notable amenity was the ice box in her galley – her champagne would remain well chilled even if she was becalmed.

In the two decades between the world wars she was often raced in the big boat class, competing against, among others, the Fife-built *Mariquita* and *Rendezvous* – both similar to her in size and design – the schooner *Westward* and the royal yacht *Britannia*.

In 1940 war once again interrupted her sailing, and like several other big yachts she was laid up in the mud in the River Hamble. After the end of World War II, *Sumurun* was modernized with an engine and resumed sailing. By 1948, her gaff rig had become obsolete and she was re-rigged as a Marconi ketch, making her easier to handle and requiring fewer hands in her crew. Unlike many of her contemporaries, she kept her name despite changing owners several times until her current owner bought her in 1980. She has since been lovingly maintained and no doubt will fulfill the prediction of an article published in *The Yachtsman* on the occasion of her launching: "So perfectly has she been put together that she looks as if she should, bar accidents, wear for, well, say a hundred years."

Sumurun is frequently seen at classic yacht events in the Mediterranean, the Caribbean and the East Coast of the United States. She was the outright winner at the 1989 Antigua Classic Yacht Regatta and has won class honors at the Vele d'Epoca in Imperia, Italy, and the Régates Royales in Cannes, France. She won the Antigua Classic again in 2002 and holds several other class wins in vintage yacht events.

That touch of scandal has almost completely faded by now as *Sumurun* approaches the century mark, although without it she would not have existed. We can thank Victoria Sackville-West, who married her first cousin Lionel, the Third Baron of Sackville, and upon inheriting a small fortune from her "gentleman friend" Sir John Murray Scott (those were certainly different times!) commissioned Fife to build *Sumurun* as a gift to her husband. As for the name? "Sumurun" means "beautiful harem girl".

74 Sumurun, *the harem beauty, reaching through the azure Caribbean waters during the Antigua Classic Yacht Regatta. She does not fly a spinnaker, but her mizzen staysail adds an extra knot of speed off the wind.*

76-77 *A dramatic photo of Sumurun, taken during the Butterfly Race at the 2010 Antigua Classic Yacht Regatta. Her distinctive knockabout bow is clearly displayed here.*

78-79 *Sumurun ahead and to windward of the staysail schooner Ashanti IV during day 4, the Windward Race, of the 2010 Antigua Classic Yacht Regatta.*

MARIETTE

- TYPE: gaff schooner
- LOA: 138 ft w/ bowsprit (42 m)
- LOD: 105 ft (32 m)
- LWL: 80 ft (24.3 m)
- BEAM: 23 ft (7.2 m)
- DRAFT: 14.5 ft (4.4 m)
- SAIL AREA: 8600 sq ft (800 sq m)
- HULL MATERIAL: steel
- DESIGNER: Nathanael Herreshoff
- BUILDER: Herreshoff Manufacturing Co., Rhode Island, USA
- YEAR BUILT: 1915
- YEAR RESTORED: 2000

Her trajectory is a familiar one for classic yachts: impeccable pedigree – commissioned by Bostonian yachtsman Frederick Brown, designed and built by Herreshoff, launched in 1915 – and an early career that was active and promising, although somewhat delayed by the outbreak of World War I. She was often sailing in company with or competing against her near sister ships, Harold Vanderbilt's *Vagrant* and Karl Trucker's *Ohonkara*. After changing owners a few times, she suffered through years of increasing neglect, only to be eventually saved and later restored to her original rig and condition.

In 1927, twelve years after her launch, *Mariette* was sold to Francis Crowninshield, who renamed her *Cleopatra's Barge* in honor of one of the first yachts ever built in America by one of his ancestors. He kept her until 1941, at which time her sailing career was once again interrupted when she was requisitioned by the United States Coast Guard and used as a patrol boat for the duration of World War II.

After the War, she was returned to Crowninshield in a substantially deteriorated condition and he reluctantly sold her. Rechristened *Gee Gee IV* by her new owner – a seemingly inappropriate name for such a lovely yacht – she began a gradual decline. Sold once again and occasionally working as a charter boat, she was eventually abandoned in a Caribbean mangrove swamp.

Mariette was saved when a group of Italian and Swiss bankers bought her in 1975 and brought her to the Mediterranean. In 1979, Italian publisher Alberto Rizzoli bought her and, giving her back her original name, commissioned a refit at Cantieri Beconcini in La Spezia. She was found to still be structurally sound, and much of the walnut paneling below decks was restored. The only major departure from the original sail plan came when she was re-rigged as a staysail schooner, a configuration which, while less authentic, was easier to handle. For about 15 years she was a familiar sight in Mediterranean harbors.

American yachtsman Tom Perkins was looking for a classic yacht to race when he noticed *Mariette* at the 1994 Nioulargue Race in St. Tropez. She changed owners one more time and immediately was sent back to Beconcini for a painstaking restoration to her original configuration. Over 150 original Herreshoff drawings were obtained from the Hart Collection at the Massachusetts Institute of Technology, new fir and spruce spars were built in England and shipped to Italy, a tiled fireplace for her main saloon was crafted in Ireland – in short, no expense was spared to bring her back to Bristol condition.

And Perkins raced her enthusiastically. *Mariette* became a welcome participant at classic yacht regattas on both sides of the Atlantic and became known as a hard-driven ship. Her trajectory has brought her back where she belongs. She has recently been sold to another passionate owner and will undoubtedly grace the classic yacht scene for years to come.

81 THE HERRESHOFF GAFF SCHOONER MARIETTE SHOWS OFF HER "LAUNDRY" AT THE 1998 ANTIGUA CLASSIC YACHT REGATTA. HERE SHE IS FLYING EIGHT SAILS GOING TO WINDWARD IN THE CARIBBEAN TRADE WINDS.

82-83 MARIETTE TEARING ALONG ON STARBOARD TACK, THROWING OFF A CLOUD OF SALT WATER SPRAY. SHE HAS TRADITIONALLY BEEN RACED HARD, AND HERE SHE CAN BE SEEN AT HER BEST, REVELING IN THE CHALLENGING CONDITIONS.

84 *Detail of* Mariette's *boom end, beautifully restored.*

84-85 Mariette *seen from the end of her bowsprit, charging along on a close reach. Her beautifully restored tender, the classic motor yacht* Atlantide, *is steaming along on her starboard quarter.*

86-87 MARIETTE'S MAIN SALOON IS A CLASSIC PERIOD TOUR DE FORCE. THE "GENTLEMEN'S CLUB" ATMOSPHERE IS TYPICAL OF EARLY 20TH CENTURY YACHTS, HERE COMPLETE WITH BRASS-FRAMED FIREPLACE, TUFTED LEATHER SETTEES AND GLASS-PANELED TROPHY CASES.

87 A STATEROOM (LEFT), FINISHED IN CLASSIC HERRESHOFF STYLE – WHITE WITH VARNISHED TRIM. ANOTHER VIEW OF THE MAIN SALOON (RIGHT), LOOKING AFT.

88-89 Mariette reaching with her asymmetrical spinnaker and gollywobbler set and drawing (the technical name for the gollywobbler is main topmast balloon staysail). Taken at the 2006 Vele d'Epoca di Imperia.

89 Sailing to windward during the Round the Island Race, at Cowes Classic Week in 2008. Mariette is setting a "mere" seven sails in this photo.

1936

TICONDEROGA

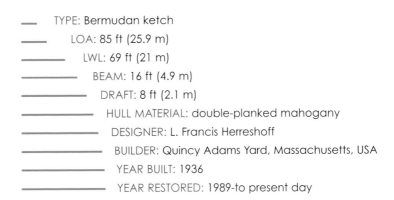

TYPE: Bermudan ketch
LOA: 85 ft (25.9 m)
LWL: 69 ft (21 m)
BEAM: 16 ft (4.9 m)
DRAFT: 8 ft (2.1 m)
HULL MATERIAL: double-planked mahogany
DESIGNER: L. Francis Herreshoff
BUILDER: Quincy Adams Yard, Massachusetts, USA
YEAR BUILT: 1936
YEAR RESTORED: 1989-to present day

*H*er launching in 1936 was a wild event. The cradle collapsed as she started down the ways and she fell off the rails. Amazingly, she sustained no damage. Originally named *Tioga*, L. Francis Herreshoff designed her for Harry Noyes, who at the time owned the Quincy Adams Yacht Yard in Quincy, Massachusetts. *Tioga* was intended to be a comfortable day sailer, although it seems that the designer/builder relationship included considerable friction over cost, commissions, building methods and eventually almost everything else about her. Notwithstanding her intended use, she proved to be a brilliant racing craft, winning 24 of the first 36 races she entered.

She was sold in 1946, after serving as a submarine patrol boat for the United States Coast Guard during World War II, and renamed *Ticonderoga*. She was given new spars, as the single spreader rig for her mainmast proved to be insufficiently strong. She then began her active career of racing and chartering. Allan Carlisle, who had bought her from the Noyes family, eventually sold her in 1951 to John Hertz Jr., who kept her until 1960. Her new owners, Baxter Still and Bill Brittain, sailed her to the Caribbean and through the Panama Canal.

She started racing on the West Coast of the U.S., winning the Transpac in 1963 and 1965, the second time setting a course record which stood for many years despite the challenges of lighter and much more modern boats. Robert Johnson was her owner at the time. He struck up a friendship with the often-difficult Herreshoff and started a long correspondence asking advice for a refit in Newport Beach. Johnson eventually donated *Ticonderoga* to Nova University, which in turn sold her to an East Coast owner.

In the early 1970s she was purchased by Ken and Fran MacKenzie, who sailed her as a charter yacht in New England and the Caribbean. They also occasionally raced her, and *Ticonderoga* continued to give a good accounting of herself. During one of their fall passages to the Caribbean they sailed her through a hurricane, somehow managing to keep her rig intact. Her decks were swept several times by green seas and her steering wheel was completely destroyed, forcing her crew to steer her into Bermuda with a pair of plumber's wrenches clamped on to the wheel shaft.

But the charter trade did not always earn enough to keep her sailing, and eventually the MacKenzies were forced to sell her. Two owners later, she was given an extensive and expensive refit in 1988 and '89 at Southampton Yacht Services, including new interior accommodations designed by John Munford. She was bought by her present owners, Scott and Icy Frantz, in 1993 and continues to ply the waters of the Caribbean and New England, her unmistakable profile easily recognized by sailors everywhere.

90 L. Francis Herreshoff's masterpiece, Ticonderoga, racing at the Antigua Classic Yacht Regatta, April 22, 2007. Sailing to windward was never her strong point, although here she seems to be bowling along happily.

92 Ticonderoga's golden eagle, patriotically carved on her transom.

92-93 The golden eagle in action, as Ticonderoga rises to the Caribbean swell during the 2007 Antigua Classic Yacht Regatta. The gleam of her topsides reflects the assiduous care devoted to her.

94-95 A GORGEOUS AERIAL PHOTO OF TICONDEROGA SAILING IN
THE CLEAR CARIBBEAN SEAS, WHERE SHE HAS BEEN A FAMILIAR AND
WELCOME SIGHT FOR OVER THIRTY YEARS. L. FRANCIS HERRESHOFF'S
LONG, DRAWN-OUT LINES ARE IN EVIDENCE AS SHE HEELS OVER.

THE J-CLASS YACHTS

ASTRA

CAMBRIA

CANDIDA

YANKEE

ENTERPRISE

SHAMROCK V

VELSHEDA

ENDEAVOUR

RAINBOW

HANUMAN

RANGER

LIONHEART

Chapter *3*

The final chapter in the history of the big classic racing sloops and cutters – the period that witnessed the apogee of their development – was written between 1930 and 1937, when the majestic J-Class sloops competed three times for the America's Cup in the United States and raced in the Big Boat Series in the United Kingdom.

The 1903 America's Cup races, convincingly won by the radical American cutter *Reliance*, clearly pointed to the need for a rating rule which would promote less extreme and safer designs. It was agreed that the next Cup challenge would be sailed under the Universal Rule, which had been adopted that year by the New York Yacht Club. The rule included a yacht's displacement in the rating formula and required that all boats designed to its specifications be built to Lloyd's A1 scantlings. The resulting boats were safer and, if not as outrageous as their giant gaff-rigged ancestors, just as magnificent.

Another significant aspect of the adoption of the Universal Rule was that it introduced level racing into big boat competition. One of the most common complaints about the America's Cup races had been that the public at large could not understand the subtleties of racing under a handicap system. It made no sense to the average spectator that one boat could cross the finish line ahead of her competitor and yet lose the race because of an unfavorable time allowance.

Boats built to the Universal Rule classes, while differing in individual design, were theoretically all capable of the same speed and thus, when racing, winners and losers were determined by the order in which they crossed the finish line. By the time *Shamrock V* arrived in America for the 1930 Cup, level racing was established.

The Americans built six J-Class sloops in the 1930s. *Whirlwind*, *Weetamoe*, *Enterprise* and *Yankee* were constructed for the 1930 America's Cup. By 1934 the Great Depression had taken a significant toll on the national economy and on personal finances, and only one new boat, *Rainbow*, was launched. *Ranger*, a "super-J" and the last of the six, defended the Cup in 1937. The British built one boat for each challenge: *Shamrock V* in 1930, *Endeavour* in 1934 and *Endeavour II* in 1937. *Velsheda* was built in 1933 for big boat racing in England and was never intended to be an America's Cup contender.

On both sides of the Atlantic, several other big boats had also been converted to J-Class rating, although strictly speaking they could not qualify as actual J-Class yachts since they were not built to Lloyd's scantlings. In America, *Resolute* and the lovely *Vanitie*, re-rigged as schooners after the 1920 America's Cup, were given Marconi rigs in 1930. In England, the 23-Metre *Astra*, *Cambria* and *Candida* were modified to rate as J-Class yachts, as were *White Heather II* and *Britannia*.

Not one of the original American boats has survived. Many of the British boats enjoyed a happier fate. Several were restored and are actively sailing now, although *Endeavour II* sadly was broken up in 1968.

Slowly at first, and then with increasing momentum, the new millennium has seen a J-Class revival. Two replicas have already launched – the new *Ranger* and *Hanuman*, which was based on *Endeavour II*. At least three more are being built: *Rainbow*, *Atlantis* (a Frank C. Paine design that had never been built) and *Lionheart* (based on one of the original *Ranger* variants). The J Class Association was formed to establish a set of bylaws regulating the class with the aim of promoting competitive and fair racing. There are basically two main rules. First, any new build must be based on original lines drawn in the 1930s and only one boat can be built to any single set of lines. Second, new boats may be built of aluminum in order to reduce the structural weight, in light of the fact that modern J-Class yachts, whether restored or new, are fitted out with complete and luxurious accommodations and carry the weight of complex machinery unimagined 70 years ago. Ironically, there has been one small retrograde step – originally intended as a level racing class, they now use a handicap when racing. That is a small price to pay when we consider their astonishing renaissance.

THE J-CLASS YACHTS

ASTRA

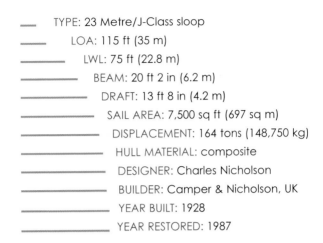

TYPE: 23 Metre/J-Class sloop
LOA: 115 ft (35 m)
LWL: 75 ft (22.8 m)
BEAM: 20 ft 2 in (6.2 m)
DRAFT: 13 ft 8 in (4.2 m)
SAIL AREA: 7,500 sq ft (697 sq m)
DISPLACEMENT: 164 tons (148,750 kg)
HULL MATERIAL: composite
DESIGNER: Charles Nicholson
BUILDER: Camper & Nicholson, UK
YEAR BUILT: 1928
YEAR RESTORED: 1987

*S*he was affectionately known as "little" Astra, the baby of the British big boat fleet. The great Charles E. Nicholson designed her as a 23-Metre sloop, and she was launched at Gosport in the United Kingdom in 1928. Her owner, Sir Adam Mortimer Singer, sailed her for just one season. She was then sold to Hugh Paul, who had her converted to rate in the J Class in 1931. After conversion to a yawl rig in 1950, she was restored to her former glory at Cantieri Navali Beconcini in 1987 and is now sailing once again as a J-Class yacht.

Those are merely the brief facts. While she could never compete for the America's Cup since 23-Metre boats were not built to Lloyd's A1 scantlings, as the Universal Rule J-Class specifications required, little *Astra* certainly could race with the best of them. She soon established a reputation for being an excellent light air sailer, occasionally beating her bigger and newer sisters.

Conversion from the 23-Metre International Rule to the Universal Rule's J Class was not an excessively difficult process for the big British sloops. It mostly involved some admittedly expensive rig changes and keel modifications to lower the maximum draft to 15 feet (5 m), the maximum allowed. Most of the 23-Metre yachts had originally been built with Marconi rigs, which further simplified the changeover.

Also facilitating *Astra*'s conversion was the fact that the British Big Boat races lasted all summer, with crews and some afterguard living on board, so all of the yachts were built with relatively complete accommodations. The 1930 American J-Class boats, on the other hand, were bare bones day sailers and stripped out for racing only, which is understandable when one considers the American philosophy – the J-Class boats were used for the America's Cup defense only (*Weetamoe* and *Yankee* were the only exceptions) and were laid up between challenges. The issue came to a head during the 1934 challenge, and eventually the J Class on both sides of the Atlantic featured properly installed accommodations.

This difference in attitudes, relevant to *Astra* as well as to her British sisters, likely explains the often-held view that the British boats were better built – whether or not they adhered to Lloyd's A1 scantlings – since they were expected to race throughout a long season and also raced every year, not just for the America's Cup challenges. While there certainly are conflicting and valid points of view on that subject, the indisputable fact is that, for whatever reason, several of the British J-Class yachts, including little *Astra*, have been lovingly restored and are still sailing, with several active in the charter trade.

When big boat racing waned after the 1937 season, Paul understood that it was the end of an era and had a 12-Metre sloop built and raced her while using *Astra* as a tender. The 12 Metre was named, appropriately, *Little Astra*.

98 ASTRA, KNOWN AFFECTIONATELY TO SAILORS AS "LITTLE ASTRA," RACING AT SOUTHEND, ENGLAND, IN 1935. THE EXTREME BEND IN HER BOOM WAS INDUCED BY THE VISIBLE LATERAL STRUTS AND STAYS AND ENHANCED THE AERODYNAMIC SHAPE OF THE FOOT OF THE MAINSAIL.

100-101 ASTRA TODAY. LIKE SEVERAL OF HER CONTEMPORARIES, SHE WAS DESIGNED AS A 23-METRE UNDER THE INTERNATIONAL RULE AND WAS MODIFIED TO RATE AS A J-CLASS YACHT. NOTE THAT SHE STILL SPORTS HER LATERAL STRUTS ON HER BOOM.

102-103 ASTRA'S MAIN SALOON IS ELEGANT YET AVOIDS SOME OF THE EDWARDIAN EXCESSES OF HER CONTEMPORARIES. THE SKYLIGHT AND PORTHOLE IMPART AN AIRY, COMFORTABLE ATMOSPHERE.

103 ASTRA'S GALLEY IS FINISHED IN WHITE, PROVIDING A PLEASANT WORKSPACE FOR HER CREW.

104-105 CANDIDA AND ASTRA *REVELING IN THE BOISTEROUS CONDITIONS OF THE* NIOULARGUE. *AL-THOUGH ORIGINALLY RENOWNED AS AN EXCELLENT LIGHT AIR PERFORMER,* ASTRA *HERE IS CLEARLY ENJOYING THE CONDITIONS, LEADING* CANDIDA *BY A BOWSPRIT LENGTH.*

CAMBRIA

TYPE: 23 Metre/J-Class Sloop

LOA: 135 ft (41.1 m)

LWL: 80 ft (24.3 m)

BEAM: 20 ft 5 in (6.2 m)

DRAFT: 13 ft (4 m)

SAIL AREA: 7,680 sq ft (713.5 sq m)

DISPLACEMENT: 162 tons (147,000 kg)

HULL MATERIAL: composite

DESIGNER: William Fife III

BUILDER: William Fife & Son, Scotland

YEAR BUILT: 1928

YEAR RESTORED: 1999

When *Cambria* and her 23-Metre sisters were launched at the beginning of the 1928 Big Boat season, there were discreet (and some not quite so circumspect) mutterings that a new breed of yachtsmen was entering the sport, people who, while they could certainly afford the game, were not quite from the proper background. Herman Andreae, whose *Candida* was launched a year later, in 1929, was a banker. *Astra* was owned by Mortimer Singer of sewing machine fame. Sir William Berry, who owned *Cambria*, was a newspaper magnate, although he did eventually acquire the proper "social credentials" when he became Lord Camrose.

Unlike the two other owners, Berry retained William Fife to design and build *Cambria*, and what a vision she was. No one would ever suggest that Charles E. Nicholson (who designed *Astra* and *Candida*) did not have an eye for beauty, but for many traditional sailors there is something about a Fife design that is unparalleled. In *Cambria's* case, however, she was very nearly paralleled – not one to be frugal when the occasion presented itself, Berry offered his wife a sister ship. Lady Camrose declined the offer, to the loss of sailing posterity.

Unlike several other big boats, including the 23 Metres, *Cambria* was not converted to rate as a J-Class yacht. Perhaps because of this, while initially successful in racing she became less competitive after the others were modified. It should be noted that when the others converted to the bigger rigs allowed by the Universal Rule, their performance improved. Also, shortly after she was launched *Cambria* had a substantial amount of ballast added, but it apparently was placed too far aft for optimal effect.

Ian Dear, in his excellent book about the J Class (*Enterprise to Endeavour*. London: Adlard Coles Nautical, 1999), observes that part of the problem may have been that more traditional sailors had been sailing on gaff-rigged yachts and did not yet know how to wring the best performance from the newly-introduced Marconi rigs. Certainly the results show that, until the new sloops were converted to J-Class rating with even more efficient, taller rigs, the older gaff-rigged boats kept right on winning races. In any case, lovely *Cambria* kept her original rig and continued competing, even if at a disadvantage. Lord Camrose sold her in 1934. She subsequently changed owners several times, eventually spending three decades in Turkey. She was re-rigged as a ketch in 1974 and sailed to New Zealand and Australia. Twenty years later she was shipped back to Cowes for further refits and eventually was given back her original sloop rig. A little more than 70 years after she was launched she finally joined the J Class and participated in many classic events, including memorably competing in the Single-Handed Race at the Antigua Classic Yacht Regatta in 2004.

Perhaps *Cambria* is still not quite competitive as a J-Class yacht when she is thrown in with restorations or replicas that sport carbon fiber rigs and molded sails, but when it's a question of sheer beauty there is simply no other in her class.

106-107 THE 135-FOOT (35 M) WILLIAM FIFE CUTTER CAMBRIA, REEFED DOWN AND CLOSE REACH-
ING ON STARBOARD TACK DURING THE 2004 ANTIGUA CLASSIC YACHT REGATTA. EXHILARATING SAIL-
ING IN PERFECT CARIBBEAN TRADE WIND CONDITIONS.

108-109 THE FOREDECK CREW ON CAMBRIA IS SETTING UP FOR A HEADSAIL CHANGE. THE AERIAL PHO-
TOGRAPH CLEARLY SHOWS THE HIGH LEVEL OF MAINTENANCE LAVISHED ON THIS TIMELESS CLASSIC YACHT.

110-111 CAMBRIA'S ELEGANT MAIN SALOON, LOOKING AFT. HER CURVED COMPANIONWAY IS SEEN
IN THE BACKGROUND. LIKE ALMOST ALL OF HER BRITISH CONTEMPORARIES, SHE WAS ORIGINALLY FITTED
OUT WITH LUXURIOUS ACCOMMODATIONS, NOW FLAWLESSLY RESTORED.

111 THE OWNER'S STATEROOM ON CAMBRIA OFFERS COMFORT AND PRIVACY.

112-113 CAMBRIA IS SAILING RAIL DOWN IN THE SOLENT DURING THE 2001 AMERICA'S CUP JUBILEE, HELD AT COWES. THE SWEEPING BEAUTY OF WILLIAM FIFE'S LINES IS DISPLAYED IN THIS PHOTOGRAPH.

113 CAMBRIA UNDER FULL SAIL. SHE IS SAILING WITH HER ORIGINAL SAIL PLAN, FLYING JIB AND ALL, AND STILL RATES AS A 23-METRE, ALTHOUGH SHE IS ALLOWED TO PARTICIPATE IN J-CLASS EVENTS.

CANDIDA

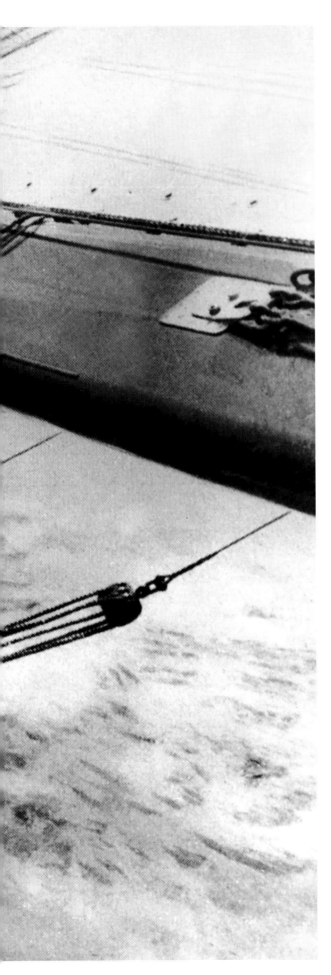

TYPE: 23 Metre/J-Class sloop
LOA: 117 ft (36.1 m)
LWL: 79 ft 9 in (24.2 m)
BEAM: 20 ft 6 in (6.2 m)
DRAFT: 13 ft 4 in (4 m)
SAIL AREA: 7,500 sq ft (697 sq m)
DISPLACEMENT: 174 tons (157,820 kg)
HULL MATERIAL: composite
DESIGNER: Charles Nicholson
BUILDER: Camper & Nicholson, UK
YEAR BUILT: 1929
YEAR RESTORED: 1989

What lovely names the Brits gave their big boats! *Britannia* – of course His Majesty's yacht could hardly be named otherwise. But then *Cambria, Astra* and *Candida*. You could imagine them as stars in a constellation, which in a sense they were – without a doubt stars of the first magnitude. It was almost as if, in 1928 and 1929, a supernova added them to the yachting firmament.

Of the three, *Candida* holds our interest not only because she was the product of the new interest in Marconi-rigged 23-Metre sloops (as were her two contemporaries) but also because of her owner, Herman Andreae, a progressive and innovative sailor in a very conservative milieu. Unlike most of his competitors – traditional owners who relied on professional skippers and mates to race their boats – Andreae was an excellent helmsman himself as well as a knowledgeable yachtsman. While one suspects that all of those Beken of Cowes photos of the various owners at the helm of their yachts were posed and destined for silver frames in their smoking rooms ashore, Andreae steered his boat when racing and personally supervised the running of his yacht.

While *Astra* excelled in light air, *Candida* loved a breeze. But while she performed well when the wind was up, the fact is that summer conditions often are mild, and while a light air boat can always reef down when the wind blows and keep racing

with some hope of success, a heavy air boat will just be slow when conditions don't suit her. *Candida's* racing performance was at first disappointing and, like the other 23-Metre big boats, Andreae had her altered to rate in the J Class.

Her modifications included fitting her with a metal mast and adding ballast. *Candida* evidently was a hard boat to steer in her favorite conditions because Andreae also had a centerboard fitted well aft to compensate for her excessive weather helm.

Her racing record remained spotty, however, and in 1934 her sail area was reduced by over 3200 square feet (300 square m) in an attempt to reduce her rating; apparently *Candida* actually rated as a 24-Metre. The other modification, temporary as it turned out, was to paint her hull gray. It had been decided that year to paint each boat sailing in the Big Boat Series a different color to help the spectators identify them. But Andreae soon had her back to her original white splendor.

By 1936 it had become obvious that she could not be made truly competitive and her owner put her up for sale. *Candida* acquired a yawl rig, was renamed *Norlanda* and continued sailing, but her racing career was over. She rejoined her rightful place in that special constellation when, in 1989, she underwent a refit that changed her back into a J-Class sloop under her proper name: *Candida*.

114-115 *Herman Andreae, the owner of Candida, is at the helm in this 1934 photograph. Unlike many contemporaries, Andreae was an expert sailor and helmsman, and personally oversaw the management of his yacht.*

116-117 *The restored Candida sailing off St. Tropez. Although originally built as a 23-metre, she now rates as a J-Class sloop after her comprehensive restoration which converted her back from her interim yawl rig.*

118 CANDIDA DRIVING INTO A WAVE AT THE NIOULARGUE, OFF ST. TROPEZ. SHE WAS ALWAYS KNOWN TO LOVE A FRESH BREEZE, AND HERE SHE IS TRULY IN HER ELEMENT.

118-119 ON BOARD CANDIDA, CLOSE HAULED UNDER REDUCED CANVAS AS SHE CLEAVES THE STEEP MEDITERRANEAN WAVES. IT IS IN CONDITIONS LIKE THESE THAT A YACHT WILL SHOW OFF HER TRUE PEDIGREE.

YANKEE

TYPE: J-Class sloop
LOA: 125 ft (38.1 m)
LWL: 84 ft (25.6 m)
BEAM: 22 ft 6 in (6.9 m)
DRAFT: 14 ft 6 in (4.4 m)
SAIL AREA: 7,288 sq ft (677 sq m)
DISPLACEMENT: 148 tons (134,240 kg)
HULL MATERIAL: Tobin bronze
DESIGNER: Frank Paine
BUILDER: Lawley, Massachusets, USA
YEAR BUILT: 1930

Of all the original American J-Class yachts, it was *Yankee* that enjoyed the longest and most active sailing career. Although she was not selected to defend the America's Cup in 1930, she gave *Enterprise*, the eventual defender, a close run for her money. Designed by Frank C. Paine for a Boston syndicate headed by John Lawrence, Charles Francis Adams and Chandler Hovey, *Yankee* was built by the renowned Lawley shipyard at Boston. She was built using Tobin bronze plating over steel frames, a technique which made for an extremely fair hull and took advantage of the natural anti-fouling properties of bronze.

Similar to several of the other J's, she had a small centerboard to help balance the helm in different wind conditions and sailing angles. And like all the other contenders she had two masts, as required by the America's Cup committee – a prudent prerequisite considering the frequency of dismastings in the J Class. Building hollow wooden masts of that length was a particularly involved process. To inspect the glue joints a small boy with a flashlight and a roller skate strapped to his back was hauled along all 170 feet (50 m) of the interior of the spar.

Yankee was commissioned again for the 1934 America's Cup defense and nearly defeated Harold Vanderbilt's new J, *Rainbow*. Her bow sec-

tions had been modified, and a new sail inventory made her faster than ever. At the time, the New York Yacht Club Cup committee was accused of favoring *Rainbow*, the New York boat, over the Boston syndicate's *Yankee*.

In 1935, American yachtsman Gerald Lambert bought her and sailed her to England to race in that summer's Big Boat Series. *Yankee*'s results were mixed, as it took Lambert some time to become used to England's fierce currents and tides as well as the more idiosyncratic use of ranges and shore landmarks for starting and finishing lines. But her performance improved as the season progressed until she lost her mast while rounding a mark during the 1935 English racing season.

Lambert had wished to remain in England for the 1936 racing season, but when a new challenge was issued for the 1937 America's Cup he did not want to be accused of staying on to spy on the new British challenger so in a gracious and sportsmanlike gesture he sent *Yankee* home. She sailed in the 1937 trials though, like all the other American boats, she was clearly outclassed by the new *Ranger*. Both boats were broken up in 1941. To acknowledge the warm welcome he had received from the British big boat fleet, Lambert sent the income from the ship breakers to Queen Mary as a contribution to the London Hospital.

121 THE J-CLASS SLOOP YANKEE, ON A PRACTICE SAIL IN BOSTON HARBOR IN 1935, IS TRYING OUT HER NEW DURALUMIN SPARS. THAT SUMMER SHE ALMOST BEAT HAROLD VANDERBILT'S RAINBOW FOR THE HONOR OF DEFENDING THE AMERICA'S CUP. IT WOULD NOT BE THE FIRST – OR LAST – TIME THE NEW YORK YACHT CLUB WOULD BE ACCUSED OF FAVORITISM.

ENTERPRISE

TYPE: J-Class sloop
LOA: 120 ft 9 in (36.6 m)
LWL: 80 ft (24.4 m)
BEAM: 23 ft (7 m)
DRAFT: 14 ft 6 in (4.4 m)
SAIL AREA: 7,580 sq ft (704 sq m)
DISPLACEMENT: 128 tons (116,100 kg)
HULL MATERIAL: Tobin bronze
DESIGNER: W. Starling Burgess
BUILDER: Herreshoff Manufacturing Co.,
Rhode Island, USA
YEAR BUILT: 1930

Of the four J-Class yachts built for the 1930 America's Cup defense, *Enterprise* was the smallest by 3 feet (1 m), with a waterline length of 80 feet (24 m). While subsequent experience proved that building to maximum length made for a faster boat, *Enterprise* made up for her size through innovation and organization. In the end, she won the right to defend the Cup after a fiercely contested round of trials against *Yankee*, and eventually she sent the British challenger, *Shamrock V*, home by winning four out of seven races.

Harold Vanderbilt, who headed the syndicate that contracted Starling Burgess to design *Enterprise*, was well known for his organizational skills. With four boats being commissioned for that year's Cup defense, it was clear that resources would be strained. Well before her keel was even laid at the Herreshoff Manufacturing Company, Vanderbilt had bought sufficient canvas for an ample sail inventory, beating his competitors who later found it difficult to order new sails. It was even rumored that he had bought up all the available bronze plating in order to delay his rivals.

The America's Cup Deed of Gift stipulated that challengers had to sail to the race venue "on their own bottom" which, considering a starting point somewhere in England, meant crossing the Atlantic under sail (in 1937 T.O.M. Sopwith was reprimanded for having had both *Endeavours* towed). As a result, *Enterprise*, like the other American boats, could be built to minimum Lloyd's scantlings as required by the J-Class rules, and it sported a completely bare-bones interior. Needless to say, *Shamrock V* was more stoutly built. It is also important to remember that while the American J-Class sloops were only sailed during America's Cup years, with *Weetamoe* and *Yankee* the only exceptions, the British boats were intended to be raced regularly with the big boat fleet in England and so were given much more comprehensive accommodations below decks.

Like all her rivals, *Enterprise* was equipped with two masts. She started the 1930 season with a wooden spar but soon stepped a revolutionary Duralumin alloy mast which weighed a mere 4000 pounds (1800 kg), or a ton less than the wood mast it replaced. Photos show an ugly 12-sided contrivance made up of aluminum plates held together by an estimated 40,000 rivets. When racing, designer Starling Burgess was assigned to keep her rig standing, which required several dedicated winches. On one windy occasion, he resorted to wrapping halyards around the shrouds to achieve sufficient tension in the standing rigging. She also sported the first Park Avenue boom, which allowed the foot of the mainsail to assume a more aerodynamic shape.

Thus equipped, and aggressively and skillfully sailed, *Enterprise* proved to be the cream of the crop in that summer of 1930. She never raced again and was broken up in 1935.

122 THE 1930 AMERICA'S CUP DEFENDER ENTERPRISE GHOSTING DOWNWIND IN LIGHT AIR. SHE IS FLYING AN OLD-FASHIONED SINGLE-LUFF SPINNAKER, WHICH WAS ACTUALLY QUITE EFFICIENT AS IT SPILLED WIND INTO HER GENOA JIB. SHE IS ALSO OBVIOUSLY HAVING SOME PROBLEMS WITH THE SPECTATORS FOLLOWING HER!

SHAMROCK V

TYPE: J-Class sloop
LOA: 119 ft 1 in (36.5 m)
LWL: 81 ft 1 in (24.7 m)
BEAM: 20 ft (6 m)
DRAFT: 14 ft 9 in (4.5 m)
SAIL AREA: 7,550 sq ft (701.5 sq m)
DISPLACEMENT: 134 tons (121,540 kg)
HULL MATERIAL: composite
DESIGNER: Charles Nicholson
BUILDER: Camper & Nicholson, UK
YEAR BUILT: 1930
YEAR RESTORED: 1968/1999

*I*f ever there is a yacht name that characterizes perseverance, it is the one given to a long sequence of majestic sloops by that exemplary good sport, Sir Thomas Lipton: *Shamrock*. Starting in 1898, the tea magnate challenged for the America's Cup no fewer than five times, building a new challenger on each occasion. The last of the series was *Shamrock V*, and we are fortunate indeed that today she is still sailing and looking better than ever.

In a way, *Shamrock V* is an anomaly among the original J-Class yachts in that she really never was retired and eventually either restored or replicated. She just kept on sailing under a succession of appreciative owners. After her unsuccessful challenge for the America's Cup in 1930, she sailed back to England. Lipton died in 1931 and she was subsequently sold to T.O.M. Sopwith, who challenged for the Cup in 1934. She was briefly owned by Sir Richard Fairey, who improved her underwater shape, rudder configuration and rig and raced her in the last of the big boat races. It is believed that she spent World War II hidden (or sunk) in Italy to prevent her lead keel from being converted into bullets.

Mario Crespi, *Shamrock V*'s next owner, refurbished her interior. After being bought by Piero Scanu, the father of the late naval architect Paolo Scanu (one of the designers of the replica of the J-Class *Ranger* launched in 2004), she enjoyed a long period of family sailing and cruising under the name *Quadrifoglio*, Italian for "four-leaf clover", the lucky shamrock.

After a refit by Camper & Nicholson in the late 1960s, she sported higher bulwarks and a larger deckhouse as well as a shortened rig for easier handling. Today we tend to be awed by the size and beauty of J-Class yachts. Paolo Scanu offered an amusing and refreshing perspective – *Shamrock V* was the family cruising boat. While everyone admired her and expressed their envy, the Scanus all complained about how much effort it took to sail her and about how narrow and uncomfortable she was compared to more modern yachts.

In 1986, Sir Thomas Lipton reached out from the past: the Lipton Tea Company bought *Shamrock V* and in a generous gesture donated her to the Museum of Yachting in Newport, Rhode Island. She was brought back to her original specifications and eventually bought by the International Yacht Restoration School, which in turn sold her to a private owner. She has since been fitted out with a carbon fiber rig and is once more competitive in today's J-Class events.

There were only two "true" J-Class yachts of composite construction: the American *Whirlwind* and *Shamrock V*; all the others were built in various combinations of steel and Tobin bronze. Of those two, *Shamrock V* is the only survivor, and she looks poised to continue her sailing and racing career for years to come.

124-125 SHAMROCK V, SLICING THROUGH A WAVE DURING THE 1999 ANTIGUA CLASSIC YACHT RE-GATTA. J-CLASS YACHTS CAN BE EXHILARATING IN THESE CONDITIONS, AS THEIR CONSIDERABLE DIS-PLACEMENT AND NARROW BEAM MAKE FOR A WET AND EXCITING RIDE.

126 SHAMROCK V IS LEADING THE FLEET DURING EARLY TRIALS FOR THE 1930 AMERICA'S CUP. CAM-BRIA CAN BE SEEN JUST ON HER STARBOARD QUARTER AND LULWORTH IS ASTERN TO THE RIGHT. THE LAT-TER TWO WERE 23-METRE YACHTS CONVERTED TO J-CLASS RATING.

127 ANOTHER RARE PHOTOGRAPH OF SIR THOMAS LIPTON SAILING ON BOARD HIS J-CLASS YACHT, SHAMROCK V. HE IS SEATED BY THE HELM, WITH GUESTS LORD INVERFORTH AND HIS TWO DAUGHTERS.

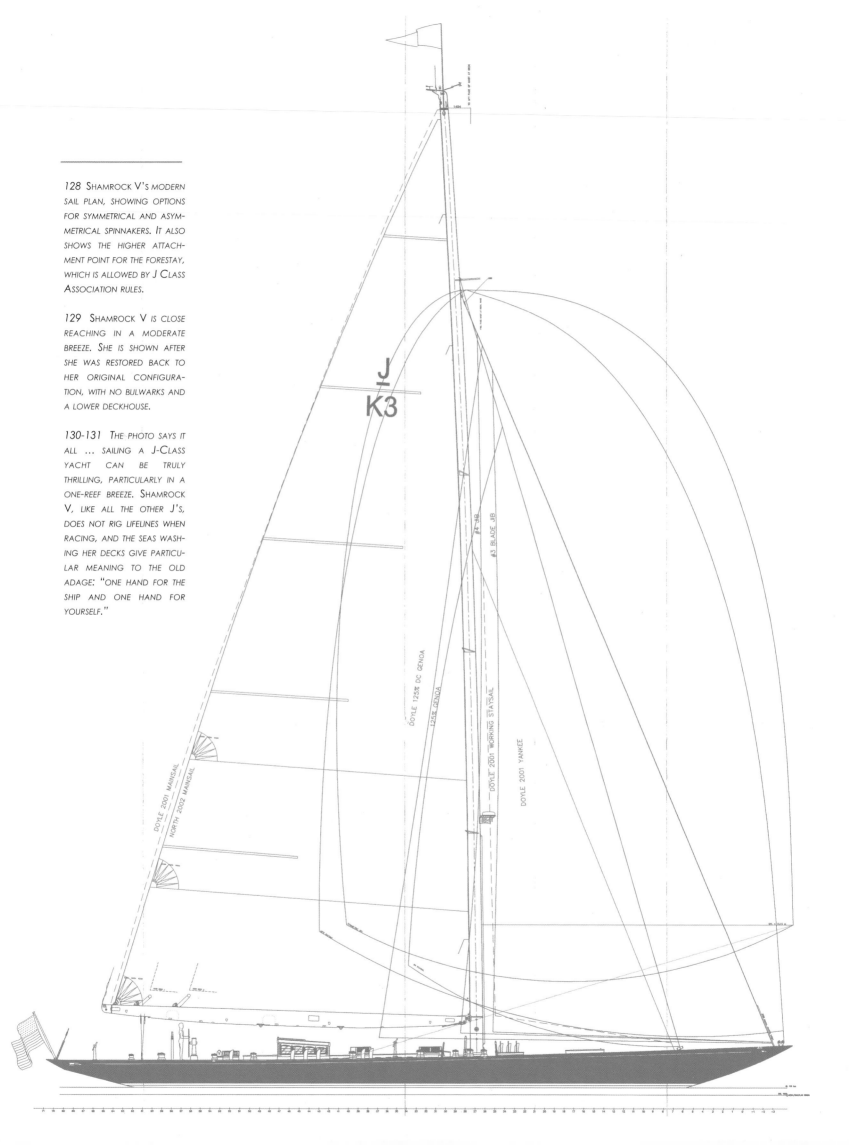

128 SHAMROCK V'S MODERN SAIL PLAN, SHOWING OPTIONS FOR SYMMETRICAL AND ASYMMETRICAL SPINNAKERS. IT ALSO SHOWS THE HIGHER ATTACHMENT POINT FOR THE FORESTAY, WHICH IS ALLOWED BY J CLASS ASSOCIATION RULES.

129 SHAMROCK V IS CLOSE REACHING IN A MODERATE BREEZE. SHE IS SHOWN AFTER SHE WAS RESTORED BACK TO HER ORIGINAL CONFIGURATION, WITH NO BULWARKS AND A LOWER DECKHOUSE.

130-131 THE PHOTO SAYS IT ALL ... SAILING A J-CLASS YACHT CAN BE TRULY THRILLING, PARTICULARLY IN A ONE-REEF BREEZE. SHAMROCK V, LIKE ALL THE OTHER J'S, DOES NOT RIG LIFELINES WHEN RACING, AND THE SEAS WASHING HER DECKS GIVE PARTICULAR MEANING TO THE OLD ADAGE: "ONE HAND FOR THE SHIP AND ONE HAND FOR YOURSELF."

J
K3

VELSHEDA

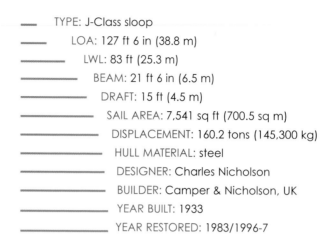

TYPE: J-Class sloop

LOA: 127 ft 6 in (38.8 m)

LWL: 83 ft (25.3 m)

BEAM: 21 ft 6 in (6.5 m)

DRAFT: 15 ft (4.5 m)

SAIL AREA: 7,541 sq ft (700.5 sq m)

DISPLACEMENT: 160.2 tons (145,300 kg)

HULL MATERIAL: steel

DESIGNER: Charles Nicholson

BUILDER: Camper & Nicholson, UK

YEAR BUILT: 1933

YEAR RESTORED: 1983/1996-7

Of all the true J-Class yachts (true in the sense that they were built to the Universal Rule and were not converted), *Velsheda* was the only one that was not built as a contender for the America's Cup. She was designed by Charles E. Nicholson and built at Camper & Nicholson for William Stephenson in 1932. *Velsheda* was named for Stephenson's three daughters – Velma, Sheila, and Daphne – a euphonious trio of names to combine into a beautiful yacht.

Although not an experienced yachtsman, Stephenson had bought the Fife 23-Metre *White Heather II* in 1929 when Lord Waring, her owner, was forced into bankruptcy. He converted her to rate in the J Class the following year, but two years later decided to build a proper J-Class boat and had *White Heather II* scrapped, using the lead from her keel and other fittings on the new boat. Unlike many of her competitors, *Velsheda* was relatively Spartan below decks, in keeping with her intended use as a day racing boat. She was rigged with a steel mast, which at the time was substantially less expensive than the newly introduced Duralumin rigs. This leads one to suspect that Stephenson either preferred to or was forced to economize. Other sources claim that she originally was equipped with an alloy spar.

Whatever Stephenson's presumed economic constraints, *Velsheda* became a staunch competitor and a frequent winner in the Big Boat class

between 1933 and 1936. As seemed to happen with alarming frequency in the J Class, she lost her mast toward the end of the 1936 season in the same race in which *Endeavour II* lost hers. Undaunted, Stephenson borrowed the spar of *Candida*, which was laid up and for sale, and kept on racing. It was to be the last glorious season for the big boats, although they kept on racing in diminished numbers for at least two more years. King George V died in 1936 and the Royal Yacht *Britannia*, which together with her royal patron had provided a great deal of the impetus behind the class, was buried at sea.

Stephenson did not commission *Velsheda* for the 1937 season, and the racing was much reduced since both *Endeavours* were across the Atlantic for the America's Cup. *Velsheda* seemed to drop out of sight. While details are vague, she was likely laid up during World War II. She spent about 25 sad years in the Hamble River mud until rescued by Terry Brabant in 1983 or 1984 (the actual date is uncertain). Brabant restored *Velsheda* to her original plain accommodations and, sailing without an engine, chartered her. A subsequent sale and interrupted refit left her neglected until she was rescued by Dutch entrepreneur Ronald de Waal in 1994. She was given a complete stem-to-stern and keel-to-truck renovation, and since 1997 she has been actively – and successfully – racing in the Mediterranean and the Caribbean.

133 VELSHEDA ROUNDING THE WINDWARD MARK AND EASING OFF TO A REACH. NOTE THE LAPPED STEEL PLATES ON HER TOPSIDES, A COMMON CONSTRUCTION METHOD WHEN THE HULLS WERE RIVETED TOGETHER.

134 FOR MANY YEARS VELSHEDA LAY IN A MUD BERTH ON THE RIVER HAMBLE, SADLY NEGLECTED.

134-135 POURING THE LEAD KEEL WAS NOT A JOB FOR THE FAINT OF HEART (OR WEAK OF BACK) IN THE 1930s. VELSHEDA'S KEEL IS BEING CAST AT CAMPER & NICHOLSON'S YARD IN SOUTHAMPTON, ENGLAND, ONE LADLEFUL OF MOLTEN LEAD AT A TIME.

136-137 THE BEAUTIFULLY RESTORED VELSHEDA RACING AGAINST THE NEW REPLICA OF RANGER AT THE ANTIGUA CLASSIC YACHT REGATTA. MOLDED SAILS, HYDRAULIC WINCHES AND CARBON FIBER SPARS MAKE THE J-CLASS YACHTS SAFER AND EASIER TO SAIL WITHOUT DETRACTING FROM THE EXCITEMENT.

138 AND 139 VELSHEDA'S CREW DOUSING HER SPINNAKER. SOME MANEUVERS STILL REQUIRE ALL HANDS TO TURN TO AND SIMPLY HAUL AWAY.

140 AND 141 TWO GORGEOUS AERIAL PHOTOGRAPHS OF VELSHEDA RACING AT THE 2005 ANTIGUA CLASSIC YACHT REGATTA. SHE HAS BEEN RACING FOR SEVERAL YEARS SINCE HER RESTORATION, AND HER CREW TRAINING IS EVIDENT BY HER PERFECTLY TRIMMED SAILS.

ENDEAVOUR

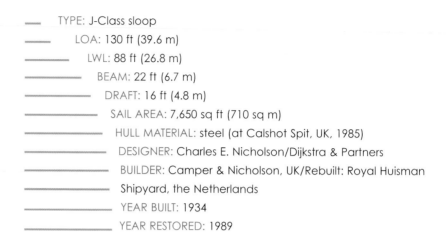

TYPE: J-Class sloop
LOA: 130 ft (39.6 m)
LWL: 88 ft (26.8 m)
BEAM: 22 ft (6.7 m)
DRAFT: 16 ft (4.8 m)
SAIL AREA: 7,650 sq ft (710 sq m)
HULL MATERIAL: steel (at Calshot Spit, UK, 1985)
DESIGNER: Charles E. Nicholson/Dijkstra & Partners
BUILDER: Camper & Nicholson, UK/Rebuilt: Royal Huisman
Shipyard, the Netherlands
YEAR BUILT: 1934
YEAR RESTORED: 1989

When T.O.M. Sopwith challenged for the America's Cup in 1934, the boat he sent across the Atlantic represented a quantum leap in design philosophy within the J Class. *Endeavour*, designed by Charles E. Nicholson and built at Camper & Nicholson in Gosport, was the most technologically advanced J-Class yacht of her time. She was the fastest J of that season as well and, to top it all off, she was absolutely lovely.

While much of the credit for her performance (she came very close to taking home the Cup) belongs to her designer, Sopwith and his engineer, Frank J. Murdoch, also deserve recognition. Their joint experience in aeronautical engineering led them to apply a scientific approach to what until then had been a largely empirical process. *Endeavour* was fitted with wind sensors and speed indicators and relied on strain gauges to monitor rigging loads.

Another innovation that showed the pair's aerodynamic expertise was the quadrilateral jib. Like most of her sister J's, *Endeavour* was sailing with a double head rig. The "quad", as it came to be known, was extremely efficient at filling the fore triangle and adding drive to the boat, a theory that had been quantified by Murdoch's strain gauges, which showed a load of two additional tons (1800 kg) on the backstay when it was set. The American

defenders lost no time in rushing to their sailmaker to have the quad copied.

In the end, the '34 Cup race boiled down to a labor problem. When *Endeavour*'s professional crew struck for higher wages, Sopwith replaced them with a crew of enthusiastic and talented amateurs. But they simply did not have the experience and practice that would enable them to race a J-Class sloop effectively. While *Rainbow*, her opponent, was widely considered the slower boat, her superior organization allowed her to barely keep the Cup in the United States.

Endeavour went back to big boat racing in England and eventually served as trial horse for Sopwith's new J, *Endeavour II*, in the 1937 America's Cup. By 1938, big boat racing was almost completely on the wane, and the onset of war forced Sopwith and Murdoch to devote all of their energy to airplane production. *Endeavour* was sold for scrap in 1947 but ultimately was spared, only to then spend the next four decades in total oblivion.

The narrative of how Elizabeth Meyer fell in love with *Endeavour* and undertook a complete restoration of her is a story for another time. But it is fair to say that Meyer's project was instrumental in launching a renewed interest in the J Class which has seen several new boats launched or under construction. The yachting world is richer for it.

143 ENDEAVOUR IS POWERED BY HER STAR-SPANGLED SPINNAKER, HER BOW WAVE CARVING UP THE OCEAN AT HULL SPEED.

144-145 JANUARY 12, 1934: THE LOWER DECK BEAMS BEING IN-STALLED ON ENDEAVOUR. STEEL HULLS WERE STILL RIVETED AND BOLT-ED TOGETHER AT THAT TIME, HENCE THE ABSENCE OF WELDING TORCHES.

146-147 THE LAUNCH OF T.O.M. SOPWITH'S J-CLASS YACHT ENDEAVOUR, THE 1934 CHALLENGER FOR THE AMERICA'S CUP. EQUIPPED WITH REMARKABLY MODERN MECHANICAL AND ELECTRI-CAL DEVICES, SHE ALMOST WON THE CUP THAT YEAR, LOSING TO HAROLD VANDERBILT'S SLOWER RAINBOW DUE TO INFERIOR OR-GANIZATION AND CREW WORK.

148 *Sir* T.O.M. *Sopwith at the helm of* Endeavour II, *looking back at the first* Endeavour.

149 Endeavour *with all downwind canvas perfectly set and drawing.* 1934 *was the last year the* J-Class *sloops used the single-luff spinnaker shown here, as parachute spinnakers proved to be far more efficient.*

150 J-CLASS SLOOPS FEEL LIKE THEY ARE POWERED BY TURBINES: ONCE THEY BUILD UP SPEED, THERE IS NO STOPPING THEM! HERE THE RE-STORED ENDEAVOUR IS SMASHING THROUGH A HEAD SEA DURING THE 1999 ANTIGUA CLASSIC YACHT REGATTA.

151 ENDEAVOUR CLOSE REACHING ON STARBOARD TACK. SAILING A J IN THESE CONDITIONS CAN BE WET WORK!

152-153 *ENDEAVOUR POWERING UPWIND OFF QUEEN CHAR-*
LOTTE ISLANDS, BRITISH COLUMBIA. UNLIKE CARIBBEAN SAILING, THE
NORTH PACIFIC WATERS CAN BE FRIGID, AS EVIDENCED BY THE AB-
SENCE OF CREW FORWARD.

154-155 *ENDEAVOUR'S MAINSHEET TRAVELER. LIKE ALL J-CLASS*
YACHTS, HER DECK GEAR IS LARGELY CUSTOM MADE, A NECESSITY
CONSIDERING THE MASSIVE STRESSES IMPOSED BY HER RIG AND
SHOCK LOADS FROM DRIVING INTO HEAD SEAS.

156-157 and 157 BELOW DECKS, ENDEAVOUR'S MAIN SALOON (LEFT) SHOWS OFF THE SUPERB JOINER WORK OF THE ROYAL HUISMAN SHIPYARD CRAFTSMEN. HALF MODELS OF J-CLASS YACHTS ARE MOUNTED ABOVE THE SETTEE, WHILE THE ACTUAL TRANSOM FROM THE ORIGINAL RANGER OVERLOOKS THE DINING AREA (ABOVE). NOTE THE CHARACTERISTIC CAMPER & NICHOLSON STAR-SHAPED DECK PRISMS.

158-159 AND 159 *ENDEAVOUR SAILING OFF SAN DIEGO AS A SPEC-TATOR DURING THE 1995 LOUIS VUITTON CUP. HERE SHE IS FLYING HER CRUISING DOUBLE HEAD RIG FOR EASE OF HANDLING.*

RAINBOW

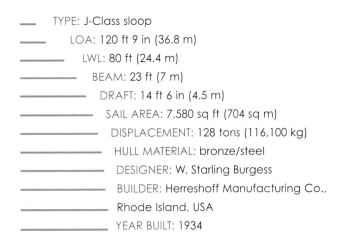

TYPE: J-Class sloop
LOA: 120 ft 9 in (36.8 m)
LWL: 80 ft (24.4 m)
BEAM: 23 ft (7 m)
DRAFT: 14 ft 6 in (4.5 m)
SAIL AREA: 7,580 sq ft (704 sq m)
DISPLACEMENT: 128 tons (116,100 kg)
HULL MATERIAL: bronze/steel
DESIGNER: W. Starling Burgess
BUILDER: Herreshoff Manufacturing Co.,
Rhode Island, USA
YEAR BUILT: 1934

*T*he 1934 America's Cup helped mark a period of transition in J-Class design, especially for the American defenders. *Rainbow*, the one new defender built that year, personified the conflicting influences at work, and she in fact came within a hair's breadth of losing the Cup to her faster rival, T.O.M. Sopwith's *Endeavour*.

The economic climate of that time made it difficult to assemble a syndicate willing to invest in such an expensive venture. Harold Vanderbilt, *Rainbow*'s skipper and the prime mover behind the effort, eventually assembled an unusually large group of 17 people. The project started late and was saved by the fact that Starling Burgess, her designer, had completed almost all the drawings for a new J two years earlier when Sir Thomas Lipton, who died shortly thereafter in 1931, had talked about yet another challenge. The Herreshoff Manufacturing Company proceeded to build her in just 100 days.

The conflict in design philosophy essentially was caused by the rapid advances in rig technology of the four previous years. The keen competition for the 1930 defense – four new boats had been built and two older yachts had been converted to rate as J's – meant that several different design solutions had been attempted. While not all were successful, some common ground was established. Double head rigs were proven to be more efficient, and the newly introduced aluminum spars could be made sufficiently strong to handle the increased loads. Some more visionary designers, notably Burgess's brother Charles, pointed out that the vastly more powerful new sail plans needed boats built to the maximum waterline length allowed by the J Class of 87 feet (26 m) in order to benefit from the added drive. But *Enterprise*, the 1930 defender, was the smallest of that vintage and had won convincingly against *Shamrock V*.

Rainbow was therefore built with a waterline length of 80 feet (24 m) and struggled for the entire season to win enough races to qualify and so to keep the Cup at home. *Yankee* had been commissioned again for the 1934 America's Cup defense by her Boston syndicate. Her bow sections had been modified and a new sail inventory made her faster than ever. She was barely beaten by *Rainbow*, and the New York Yacht Club Cup committee was accused of favoring the New York boat.

Vanderbilt and *Rainbow* went on to successfully defend the America's Cup after losing the first two races. Ironically, *Rainbow*, the shortest of the American J's, later proved Charles Burgess correct. Vanderbilt bought her from the syndicate in 1936 and added 10 tons (9000 kg) of lead to her keel, bringing her down on her lines to an 87-foot (26 m) waterline length. The extra weight made her even faster, paving the way for her maximum-length successor, the "super J" *Ranger*.

Rainbow was scrapped in 1940 and today, 70 years later, her replica, designed by Dijkstra & Partners and built at Holland Jachtbouw in the Netherlands, is about to be launched, a fitting tribute to a pivotal yacht.

160 HAROLD VANDERBILT'S RAINBOW, RACING DURING THE 1934 AMERICA'S CUP DEFENSE TRIALS. J-CLASS YACHTS WERE ALL SAILING WITH DOUBLE HEAD RIGS BY THEN, AS SHOWN IN THIS PHOTO. THE J TO WINDWARD AND AHEAD OF RAINBOW IS THE BOSTON SYNDICATE'S YANKEE.

162 THE 1934 AMERICA'S CUP DEFENDER RAINBOW SAILING IN THE FIRST SET OF TRIAL RACES OFF NEWPORT, RHODE ISLAND. THIS PHOTOGRAPH APPEARED IN THE ILLUSTRATED LONDON NEWS IN JUNE OF THAT YEAR – SURELY AN INDICATION OF THE PUBLIC INTEREST IN T.O.M. SOPWITH'S FIRST CHALLENGE.

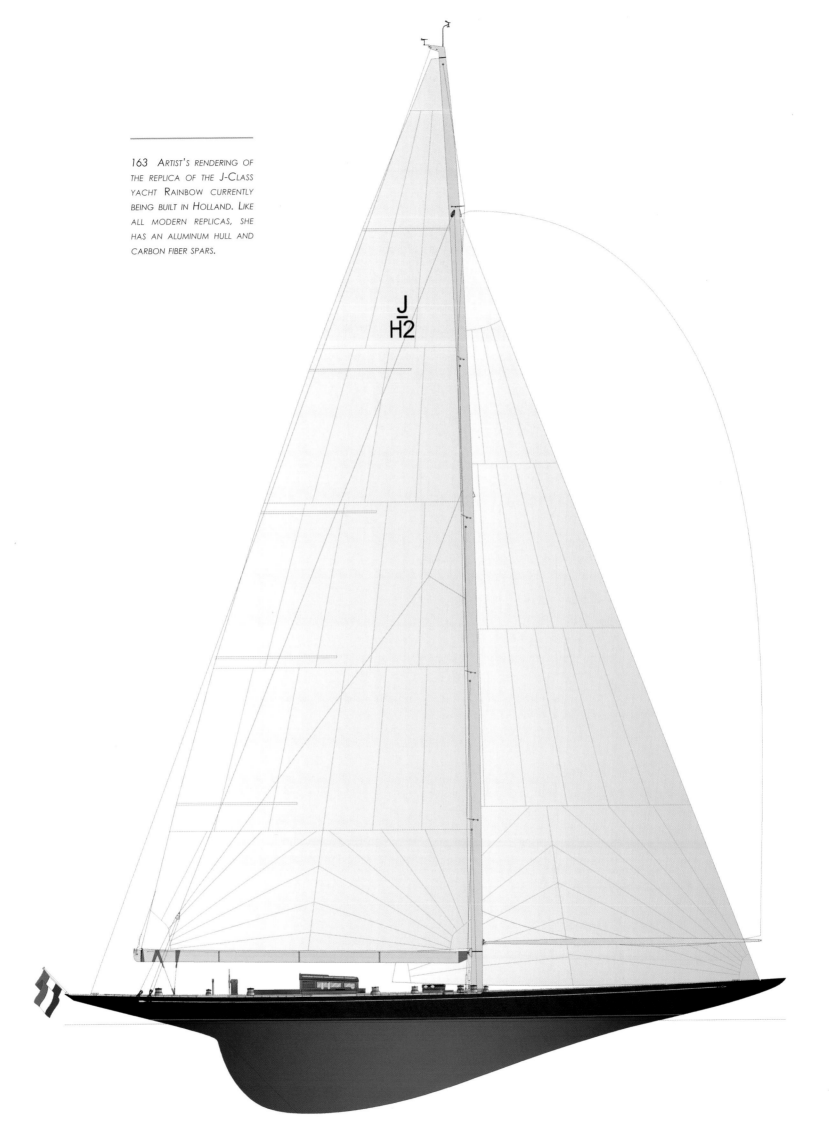

163 ARTIST'S RENDERING OF
THE REPLICA OF THE J-CLASS
YACHT RAINBOW CURRENTLY
BEING BUILT IN HOLLAND. LIKE
ALL MODERN REPLICAS, SHE
HAS AN ALUMINUM HULL AND
CARBON FIBER SPARS.

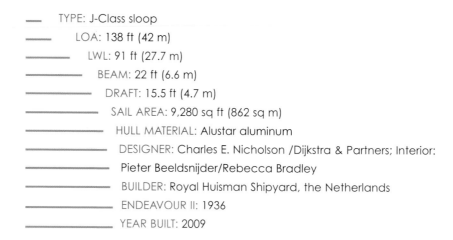

— TYPE: J-Class sloop
— LOA: 138 ft (42 m)
— LWL: 91 ft (27.7 m)
— BEAM: 22 ft (6.6 m)
— DRAFT: 15.5 ft (4.7 m)
— SAIL AREA: 9,280 sq ft (862 sq m)
— HULL MATERIAL: Alustar aluminum
— DESIGNER: Charles E. Nicholson /Dijkstra & Partners; Interior: Pieter Beeldsnijder/Rebecca Bradley
— BUILDER: Royal Huisman Shipyard, the Netherlands
— ENDEAVOUR II: 1936
— YEAR BUILT: 2009

*I*t must be difficult for owners of mere superyachts. They can devote endless time and resources to having yet another "ultimate" yacht built, only to then be overshadowed by the ever-increasing ranks of huge sailing craft.

Not so for the owners of new J-Class yachts. Talk about instant cachet – not only do they own a magnificent classic complete with all the advantages of modern materials and technology, but perhaps more importantly they also own a major piece of yachting history.

Hanuman is a case in point. When Jim Clark decided to commission a new J, he started at the end of the J-Class evolutionary ladder. A replica of *Ranger* had already been built. Although there were six more alternative sets of *Ranger* lines available, Clark opted for her old antagonist, *Endeavour II*. Charles E. Nicholson's 1936 challenger was lovely, big and certainly fast – very likely as fast as *Ranger*, although not as well sailed. Today's J Class Association rules and modern technology make those comparisons essentially irrelevant anyway.

Hanuman (named after the Hindu monkey god representing strength and perseverance) is the first of the J-Class replicas to be built of aluminum. Almost all of the 1930s J's, as well as the *Ranger* replica launched in 2004, were built of steel. While the considerable weight savings ideally would be incorporated into the ballast, the reality is that much of it is actually used up by the requisites of modern sail-

ing. If years ago, as the expression goes, ships were made of wood and the men who sailed them were made of iron, these ships are made of Alustar and the men and women who sail them must have hot water, air conditioning, ice for their rum and hydraulics to turn the winches.

In choosing a builder for *Hanuman*, Clark didn't hesitate. He returned to the Royal Huisman Shipyard, which had previously built the 155-foot (47 m) sloop *Hyperion* and the 260-foot (78 m) three-masted schooner *Athena* for him. Huisman enjoys a stellar reputation as a yacht builder. They are renowned for their quality and meticulous attention to detail. In addition, they provide a sort of superyacht one-stop shopping resource, rigging and equipping their builds with spars and hardware from their proprietary Rondal facility.

Credit for creating a J-Class replica like *Hanuman* spans decades: her inspiration, *Endeavour II*, was designed by Nicholson in 1936. But within the parameters set by the original lines, Dijkstra & Partners, naval architects based in Amsterdam, had to create a 21st century sailing yacht while taking advantage of the most up-to-date technology available. Furthermore, it took the painstaking talent of interior designer Pieter Beeldsnijder to give her the kind of accommodations that were unheard of back in 1936.

All that talent and a sailor's vision: *Hanuman* is a floating evocation of yachting history. With all due respect to Clark, who provided the vision, in a sense she belongs to all sailors.

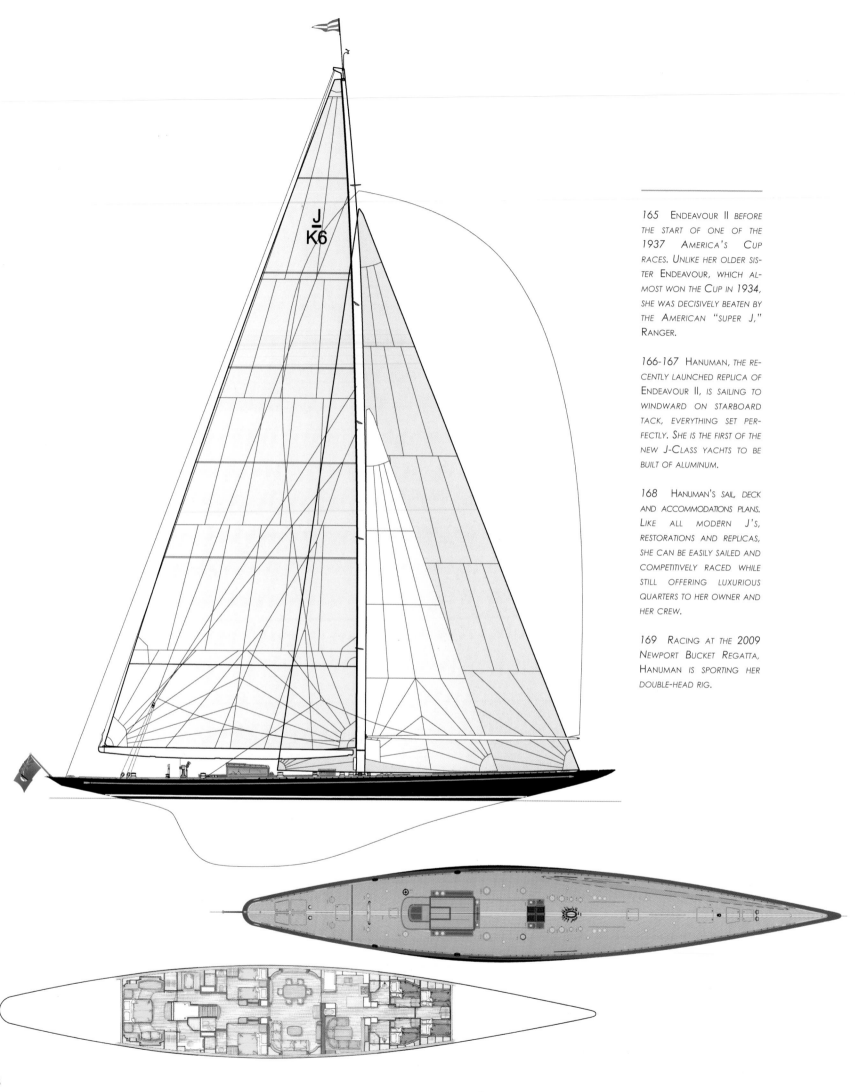

165 ENDEAVOUR II *BEFORE THE START OF ONE OF THE 1937* AMERICA'S CUP *RACES. UNLIKE HER OLDER SISTER* ENDEAVOUR, *WHICH ALMOST WON THE CUP IN 1934, SHE WAS DECISIVELY BEATEN BY THE AMERICAN "SUPER J,"* RANGER.

166-167 HANUMAN, *THE RECENTLY LAUNCHED REPLICA OF* ENDEAVOUR II, *IS SAILING TO WINDWARD ON STARBOARD TACK, EVERYTHING SET PERFECTLY. SHE IS THE FIRST OF THE NEW J-CLASS YACHTS TO BE BUILT OF ALUMINUM.*

168 HANUMAN'S *SAIL, DECK AND ACCOMMODATIONS PLANS. LIKE ALL MODERN J'S, RESTORATIONS AND REPLICAS, SHE CAN BE EASILY SAILED AND COMPETITIVELY RACED WHILE STILL OFFERING LUXURIOUS QUARTERS TO HER OWNER AND HER CREW.*

169 *RACING AT THE 2009* NEWPORT BUCKET REGATTA, HANUMAN *IS SPORTING HER DOUBLE-HEAD RIG.*

170-171 HANUMAN'S DINING AREA, PART OF HER MAIN SALOON. CONSIDERING THAT THE OWNERS OF THE ORIGINAL J-CLASS YACHTS LIKELY NEVER SPENT A NIGHT ABOARD, TODAY'S OWNERS CERTAINLY CAN LIVE LARGE!

171 HANUMAN'S ELEGANTLY EQUIPPED SALOON, AN INDISPENSABLE PART OF J-CLASS SAILING.

172 *Passageway facing aft, with a statuette of the god Hanuman prominently displayed.*

173 *A comfortable stateroom on board the J-Class yacht Hanuman.*

174 *After a mark rounding aboard the J-Class sloop Hanuman. The asymmetrical spinnaker is set and drawing and the foredeck crew is handing the forestaysail.*

175 *Hanuman sailing to windward on Day 1 of the 2010 Newport Bucket Regatta.*

RANGER

There were, unquestionably, more beautiful J-Class yachts, but of all the J's ever built – modern replicas as well the original 1930s fleet – none captured the sailing world's imagination as much as *Ranger*. Perhaps it was her brilliant meteoric career. She won every match race she sailed – 35 of them – and suffered only two losses, both in fleet racing, in the five months which comprised her entire sailing career from launch to the final trip to the ship breaker's yard. Certainly, back in 1937 she represented the culmination, and the end, of an era.

But *Ranger* also represented a transition in yacht design, from a more empirical and evolutionary (not to mention artistic) approach to the application of objective, quantifiable information scientifically obtained. Her design team, consisting of W. Starling Burgess and Olin J. Stephens II, developed six alternative sets of lines (a seventh set was later discovered) which were exhaustively tank-tested at the Stevens Institute of Technology in Hoboken, New Jersey. The consistent winner, model 77-C, became *Ranger*.

"...The fact is that Ranger was the product of a country that was moving into the new scientific era while Endeavour II [the British challenger] was the product of a country still thinking of yacht design as an art ... with tank testing Stephens and Burgess had used science – not their artistic intuition – as their guide to choosing the defender's lines." (from *Enterprise to Endeavour*, by Ian Dear. London, Adlard Coles Nautical, 1999.)

She was built in the depths of the Depression over the winter of 1936-37 at Bath Iron Works in Maine. There was no written contract, just a handshake agreement between Harold S. Vanderbilt and Bath Iron Works President William S. Newell, and she was built at cost in just 140 days. Admittedly, that remarkably short build time was made possible by the fact that she had no engine, a primitive galley for her crew, only basic accommodations to meet the class requirements and no machinery at all.

With the modern-day interest in the J Class and no older boats available to restore, American yachtsman John Williams decided to build a new J-Class yacht. And, not surprisingly, he felt that his best option was to build a replica of model 77-C, *Ranger*.

Impeccably built and exquisitely finished by Danish Yacht in Skagen, Denmark, she has been turning heads wherever she sails. While faithful to the lines of the original, she is thoroughly modern. A carbon fiber rig, hydraulic winches and aramid running rigging all contribute to her thrilling performance. Below decks she offers every comfort available to modern yachts, all within a gorgeous varnished context. Times have indeed changed, and the new *Ranger* has set the standard for all of the new J-Class yacht replicas that follow.

176-177 The new Ranger clearly relishing the Caribbean trade winds during the 2004 Antigua Classic Yacht Regatta, which was her racing debut three months after her launching in Denmark. The white water on deck is typical of J-Class yachts in breezy conditions.

178-179 Ranger, the "super J," on an early practice sail a month after her launch in 1937. She had stepped her replacement Duralumin mast three days previously. Her distinctive snub bow did not appear in her drawings, but was changed during the construction process.

179 Harold S. Vanderbilt looking aloft at Ranger's sails while at the helm during the 1937 America's Cup defense trials. Note the flexible riveted aluminum boom behind him.

180-181 The new Ranger close hauled during the 2004 Antigua Classic Yacht Regatta. Her signature bow was perfectly replicated in the new boat.

182-183 The main saloon of the new Ranger. A far cry from her predecessor's Spartan quarters, the leather upholstery and foam core varnished mahogany panels are typical of today's J-Class yachts.

183 Ranger's deckhouse (left), looking forward, and her owner's stateroom (right).

184-185 Ranger sailing off Palma de Majorca in the Superyacht Cup Ulysse Nardin, June 2007.

LIONHEART

- TYPE: J-Class sloop
- LOA: 142 ft (43.3 m)
- LWL: 87 ft (26.5 m)
- BEAM: 21.5 ft (6.5 m)
- DRAFT: 15 ft (4.5 m)
- HULL MATERIAL: aluminum
- DESIGNER: Hoek Design Naval Architects
- BUILDER: Hull built by Bloemsma BV/
- Claasen Jachtbouw BV, the Netherlands
- YEAR BUILT: 2010

With *Lionheart*, the modern J Class era is entering a sort of ideological *terra incognita*. All the J-Class yachts sailing today are restorations of actual Js (*Shamrock V*, *Endeavour*, and *Velsheda*), old 23-Metre yachts converted to J-Class rating (*Astra*, *Cambria*, and *Candida*) or replicas of J's that actually were built and sailed back in the 1930s (*Ranger* and *Hanuman*.)

Of the 20 J-Class sloops designed in the 1930s, 10 were actually built and sailed. Of those, only 3 survive and have been restored. Any new J-Class yacht must be built to an original set of lines, which leaves J-Class enthusiasts contemplating the fact that they could see as many as 15 new boats built.

What makes *Lionheart* particularly interesting, therefore, is that she is the first new J-Class yacht to be built to lines that were never originally used. Starling Burgess and Olin Stephens developed seven sets of lines for *Ranger*, the 1937 America's Cup defender, and it is to these lines that Dutch naval architect Andre Hoek turned when asked to develop a new J. In these post tank-testing days, velocity prediction programs enable us to calculate with a high degree of precision the behavior of a yacht based on a computer analysis of her lines. Hoek chose model 77-F, the set of *Ranger* lines which offered the best all-around performance.

The fact that *Lionheart*, unlike the other replicas, has no predecessor is actually of little consequence to her potential. Modern construction techniques and materials – Alustar hulls, carbon fiber rigs and aramid rigging, molded sails – allow designers to optimize a J in ways that were simply unavailable when she was originally designed. Also significant is the fact that Hoek has made a specialty of designing modern classics and is knowledgeable about sweeping lines, long overhangs and sweet sailing.

He also knows, one might add, how to give a yacht all the requisite characteristics, from structural strength and safety to expertly designed sail-handling systems. After the hull was completed at Freddie Bloemsma's shipyard, *Lionheart* was moved to Claasen Jachtbouw for finishing – a frequently used process in superyacht builds which require the extensive experience of specialists to realize the required level of detail.

Not surprisingly, the fact that *Lionheart*, like all modern J-Class yachts, is expected to be capable of world-wide cruising as well as occasional day racing means that, while her hull design faithfully adheres to the lines of Burgess and Stephens, she is a far cry from what she might have been like back in 1937. Her latter-day designers have given her a luxurious and complete cruising interior, enhanced by such amenities as a private owner's deckhouse and a cockpit aft of the helm.

It took 73 years to finally build *Lionheart* and for her finally to be welcomed into the J Class. It is a tribute to her timeless design that she looks right at home.

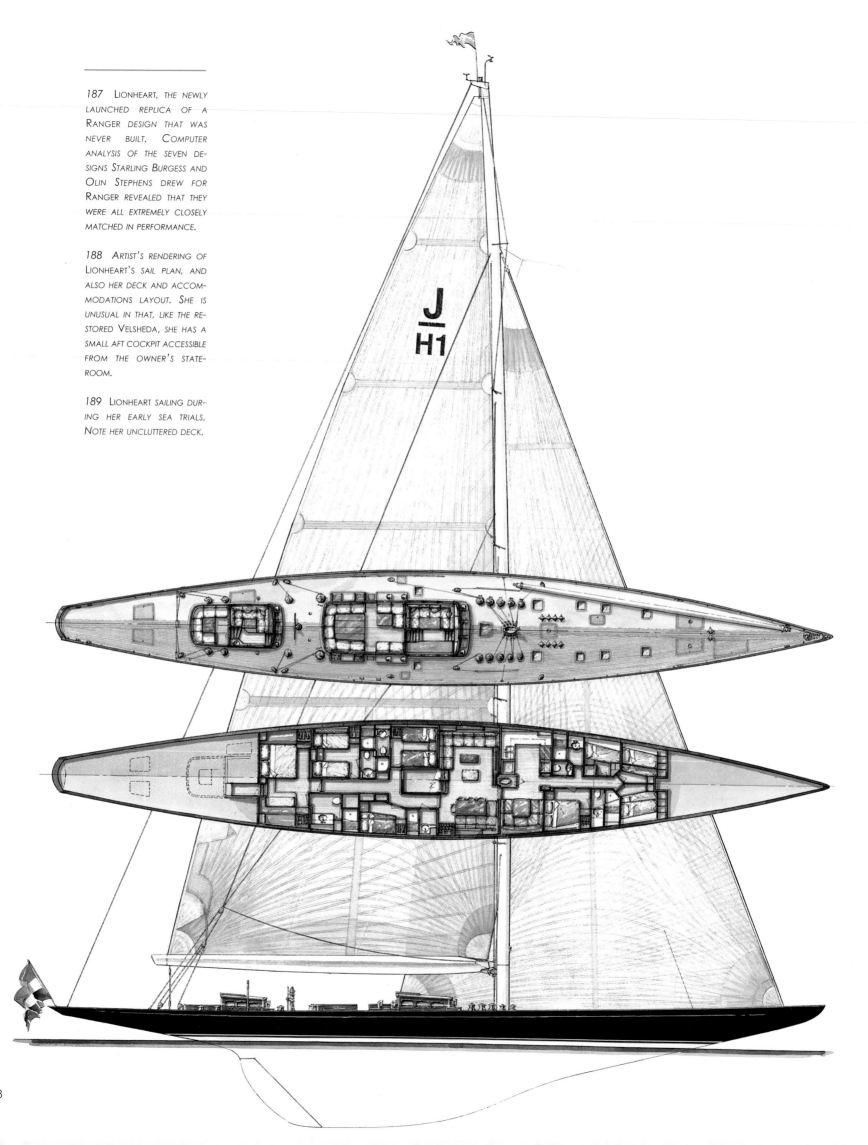

187 LIONHEART, THE NEWLY LAUNCHED REPLICA OF A RANGER DESIGN THAT WAS NEVER BUILT. COMPUTER ANALYSIS OF THE SEVEN DESIGNS STARLING BURGESS AND OLIN STEPHENS DREW FOR RANGER REVEALED THAT THEY WERE ALL EXTREMELY CLOSELY MATCHED IN PERFORMANCE.

188 ARTIST'S RENDERING OF LIONHEART'S SAIL PLAN, AND ALSO HER DECK AND ACCOMMODATIONS LAYOUT. SHE IS UNUSUAL IN THAT, LIKE THE RESTORED VELSHEDA, SHE HAS A SMALL AFT COCKPIT ACCESSIBLE FROM THE OWNER'S STATEROOM.

189 LIONHEART SAILING DURING HER EARLY SEA TRIALS. NOTE HER UNCLUTTERED DECK.

THE MODERN CLASSICS

Chapter *4*

*I*t may be a matter of prejudice, but you could wager with a reasonable degree of assurance that, seventy years from now, nobody will ever want to build a replica of a modern IRC boat (or a monohull that has been handicapped for racing), a Vendée Globe ocean racer or, for that matter, even a contemporary fiberglass production sailboat. Furthermore, modern mega-sailing yachts will not likely find many imitators. And yet today we have a well-established market for restored yachts from the first half of the 20th century, and boat yards are busy restoring and building replicas of those yachts.

One of the tests for determining whether a boat deserves to be considered a classic is simple: She has to make you want to turn around and look back when you get in the dinghy to go ashore. No one, unless they are worried about the anchor holding, ever looks back at a chartered bareboat.

While aesthetics are key to the appeal of the classics, it is also a fact that many of those old classics were a delight to sail. To be sure, there were also many that were cranky, slow and even unseaworthy. Some, dare we say it, were not even particularly pretty. The advantage of our retrospective point of view is that the cranks have been winnowed out by time while the beauties have remained.

Obviously, those classic yachts built fifty or more years ago are a finite resource. Many of the ones that survived (and a gratifying number of them did) have been well maintained or restored and are being enjoyed by appreciative owners. Sailors who appreciate the intrinsic characteristics of these yachts and also want to own and enjoy them have created a parallel, and no less valid, world of classic replicas – boats which either duplicate existing lines or are original designs in what is termed "the spirit of tradition."

There is no room for snobbism here. While die-hard purists may raise an eyebrow at the thought of a replica built using composite technology and rigged with carbon fiber spars, the fact remains that these are yachts which give us the aesthetic and tactile experience of sailing a classic while offering affordable maintenance and unmatched safety. They should be welcome into the fraternity of classic yachts and enjoyed in the spirit in which they were created.

SIGNE

TYPE: ketch

LOA: 115 ft (35 m)

LWL: 93 ft (28.3 m)

BEAM: 22 ft (6.7 m)

DRAFT: 22 ft (6.7 m)

HULL MATERIAL: WEST system/cold-molded

DESIGNER: Bruce King Yacht Design/interior:

Joseph Artese Design

BUILDER: Renaissance Yachts, Maine, USA

YEAR BUILT: 1990

YEAR RESTORED: 2004/2005

*I*f proof is needed that there is a common thread in classic yacht design, a sort of genealogical descent from a common trunk, just look at lovely *Signe*. She is Bruce King's fourth in a series of yachts inspired by L. Francis Herreshoff, with a clipper bow, 15-foot (5 m) bowsprit and wineglass varnished transom reminiscent of the latter's seminal *Ticonderoga*. Her owners had admired two of King's earlier creations, *Whitehawk* and *Whitefin*, and decided to have their boat built (appropriately in this context of modern classics) by Renaissance Yachts in Thomaston, Maine.

Signe's owners at first wanted her built traditionally, using plank-on-frame construction. This was rejected in favor of cold-molded construction using WEST SYSTEM epoxy, resulting in a much stronger and stiffer hull capable of handling the significant tension generated by her tall rig. King specified longitudinal mahogany inner and outer skins, with three layers of diagonally-oriented cedar as a core. Although her owners would have preferred wooden spars, their choice of in-mast furling for the main and mizzen dictated the use of aluminum for the masts, but they were able to retain wooden booms.

Tradition and classic appearance were of primary importance. However, *Signe*'s owner, designer and builder were not fanatical in their approach, and modern technology was applied liberally. The accommodations were designed by Joseph Artese, who was instrumental in developing the polyhedral skylights which have become a King signature. *Signe*'s skylight is a decahedron with beveled glass panes that shower refracted light below deck. In fact, light is everywhere. There are 17 opening deck hatches, numerous opening ports and a remarkable 32 deadlights and deck prisms.

Signe's interior space is an exquisite series of curved counters and arched doorways, while the cambered deck beams overhead are set off by vestigial hanging knees. Hawaiian koa wood is primarily used, with accents in bird's-eye maple and burled olive – the latter surely an unusual wood on a yacht. In keeping with King's philosophy that a boat's structure should be part of her aesthetic impact, the main backstay is visible where it is led below deck to a bronze keel mounted support, as are her main chainplates in the guest staterooms and captain's cabin. In a structural and visual *tour de force*, the mizzen mast uses as partners the nonagonal skylight in the owner's stateroom.

Signe was named after the Danish grandmother of one of her owner's, who had lived to be a hundred years old, and it was built as an intended future retirement home. The owners eventually sold her and she has been active in the charter trade since then, sailing in the Mediterranean, the Caribbean and United States East Coast. A complete refit in 2004 and 2005 has kept her in Bristol condition, always a lovely sight with her distinctive elliptical deckhouse and cockpit.

192 *A FISH EYE VIEW OF THE KETCH* SIGNE *LIFTING TO THE OCEAN SWELL. IN KEEPING WITH TRADITION, HER BOWSPRIT IS CAPPED WITH WHITE PAINT.*

194-195 *THE BRUCE KING-DESIGNED KETCH* SIGNE *IS SAILING UNDER REDUCED CANVAS AT THE* SUPERYACHT CUP REGATTA. *SHE IS ONE OF A SERIES OF NEO-CLASSIC CREATIONS FROM HER DESIGNER'S BOARD. THIS PHOTOGRAPH CLEARLY SHOWS OFF THE ELLIPTICAL DESIGN MOTIF ON DECK.*

HETAIROS

TYPE: ketch
LOA: 140.5 ft (42.8 m)
LWL: 100 ft (30.5 m)
BEAM: 28 ft (8.5 m)
DRAFT: 28.5 ft/10 ft w/ board up/board down (8.7 m/3 m
board up/down)
HULL MATERIAL: Mahogany cold-molded
DESIGNER: Bruce King Design/interior:
Andrew Winch Design
BUILDER: Abeking & Rasmussen, Germany
YEAR BUILT: 1993

*H*etairos is most definitely a new classic. Designed by Bruce King, who has a distinct penchant for traditional lines, *Hetairos* – with her low freeboard, sweeping sheer and raked masts – is an exquisite example of how modern materials and engineering can work to create an aesthetic ideal. It is rare to find someone who would choose to build a wooden boat the size of *Hetairos*. Her owner had formerly owned a 65-foot (20 m) Henry Scheel design built in aluminum, but when he decided to build his dream boat he opted for cold molded construction.

Years of research went into the final brief, and the building contract was eventually awarded to Abeking & Rasmussen in Lemwerder, Germany, where *Hetairos* was launched in 1993. Her hull was made up of six layers of mahogany sheathed in fiberglass and painted jet black with a traditional gold-leaf cove. The hull was built up on laminated frames and stringers, and the teak deck was laid on laminated deck beams. Deck trim is varnished teak. The effect, as the owner has been known to repeatedly point out, is that *Hetairos* is his vision of a "symphony in wood."

She is simply breathtaking, whether at anchor, under sail or even moored stern to a dock. And below decks she is even more impressive, if that's possible. The interior is yet another of Andrew Winch's masterpieces, evoking the between-the-wars era when yacht accommodations were elegant replicas of the homes of their owners, who liked their fa-

miliar comfort and needed no reminder that they were afloat. The navigation station, properly located in the deckhouse halfway down the companionway, is all mahogany and leather and is more club-like than nautical.

The main saloon, besides being an evident tribute to Abeking & Rasmussen's craftsmen, is a striking exhibition of her designer's nautical sensibility. In his plans, King states unequivocally that: "The deck beams are the deck beams. The underside of the deck is just that; no suspended ceilings or other covers to hide wires, plumbing, and other visual unpleasantness... Much of the structure must be visually attractive as well as be integrated with the overall aesthetic design of the total yacht." The massive laminated beams that span the entire width of the saloon are the perfect manifestation of his philosophy. The traditional chamfered planks of the overhead are an additional enhancement. And of course, no King yacht would be complete without his signature polygonal skylight.

A dreamboat by any standard, *Hetairos* was not just built to look pretty – she was meant for sailing and for long passages. By the end of her first year she had already been halfway around the world, to Antarctica by way of the South Pacific. She is currently very active sailing the various classic regattas in the "spirit of tradition" class and is also a regular at the Bucket regattas. She may not be old enough to be a legendary classic, but she has certainly gotten off to a good start.

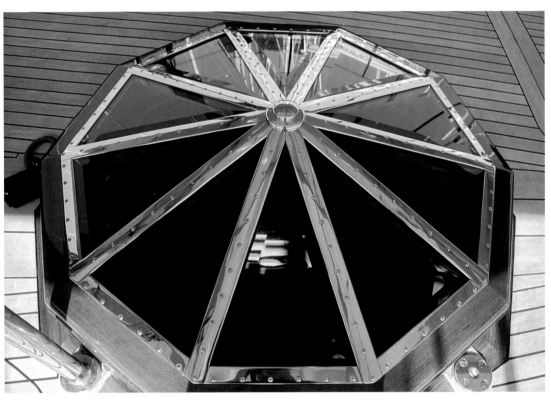

196-197 *Hetairos is charging along under full sail. From her carved and gold-leafed trailboards atop her clipper bow to her elliptical transom, she encompasses the best of two worlds: elegant traditional aesthetics with all the benefits of modern technology.*

198-199 *This dramatic photograph of Hetairos under full sail perfectly conveys the excitement of sailing a modern classic: she looks gorgeous, is truly in her element and her crew clearly is relishing the thrill.*

200-201 *The master stateroom (left) on Hetairos is finished in a classic combination of varnish and white paint. Overhead is designers Bruce King's and Joseph Artese's signature polygonal skylight.*

201 top *A masterful carving, typical of the many exquisite details aboard Hetairos.*

201 bottom *The decagonal skylight as seen from above. The glass panels reflect faceted light in constantly varying patterns.*

202-203 *Hetairos is dowsing her huge asymmetrical spinnaker during a light air race. The reflection of her bow wave on her topsides shows off her flawless hull finish.*

WILD HORSES and WHITE WINGS

TYPE: sloop
LOA: 76 ft (23.2 m)
LWL: 54 ft (16.4 m)
BEAM: 16 ft (4.8 m)
DRAFT: 11 ft (3.3 m)
SAIL AREA: 2,239 sq ft (208 sq m)
HULL MATERIAL: cold-molded red cedar and Douglas-fir
DESIGNER: Joel White
BUILDER: Brooklin Boat Yard and Rockport Marine,
Maine, USA
YEAR BUILT: 1998/1999

Sister ships *White Wings* and *Wild Horses*, the two ubiquitous W-76 sloops, have been turning heads for well over a decade, often appearing as a matched set at various classic yacht regattas in the United States, the Caribbean and Europe. They were built almost simultaneously by two neighboring Maine boat yards in 1998 – Brooklin Boat Yard and Rockport Marine – from the last design of the late Joel White. They were commissioned by Donald Tofias, a classic yacht enthusiast who dreamed of bringing back the days of level racing in big boats.

White's love for beauty, tradition and simplicity is evident everywhere aboard. The W-76's long overhangs may seem like an anachronism today, but they establish the classic character of the boat. The sharp, slightly hollow entry at the waterline sweeps aft to a perfect wine-glass transom, the whole tied together by a flawlessly-drawn sheer line. As an architect, White was never too proud to borrow from past masters while still making his designs uniquely his own; the W-76 surely owes a debt to the great Nathanael Herreshoff above the waterline.

Underwater, however, her intended use as a day racer becomes apparent. Like many modern classics, she sports a bulb keel and spade rudder, and why not? She is livelier because of it and still lovely to look at. The symbiosis of modern functionality and traditional aesthetics is evident on deck as well. Her deckhouse, with its vertical sides and rectangular deadlights, could have been lifted from a vintage R-boat or a New York 40. Her cockpit, all teak and varnish, sports winch pedestals and all the modern requisites for efficient sail handling. Carbon fiber spars and state-of- the-art sails enhance her performance without detracting from her classic appearance.

Simplicity and practicality is evident below decks as well. There is a comfortable cabin for her permanent crew, ample sail stowage and a lovely and roomy main saloon. All are finished in varnished cherry with many traditional touches. There is no owner's stateroom at all. Instead, in keeping with her classic role evoking the early 20th century 12 Metres, M-sloops and NY 50s, which all were mainly used as day racing boats, the owner is expected to sleep in comfort ashore.

A further advantage to building a contemporary classic is the availability of modern materials. Cold-molded construction, as used in the W-76, employs epoxy resin (certainly not available to Mr. Herreshoff) as well as techniques which ensure an immensely strong, rigid and long-lasting boat. Purists may object, but there is a lot to be said for a boat which will not leak or suffer from compression loads.

It is, after all, a matter of adhering to the spirit of the concept of a classic yacht and not so much to the letter of it, especially if blindly following now-obsolete techniques results in additional maintenance and concern. The W-76s manage a balance between a truly classic and traditional appearance and finish combined with techniques afforded by modern materials and systems. They are beautiful and they are fun – who could ask more of a sailing yacht?

204 THE W-76 SLOOP WILD HORSES SAILING ON PORT TACK WITH HER CREW LINED UP ON THE RAIL DURING THE 2001 ANTIGUA CLASSIC YACHT REGATTA. SHE AND HER SISTER SHIP WHITE WINGS ARE A FREQUENT AND POPULAR SIGHT AT CLASSIC YACHT REGATTAS EVERYWHERE.

206-207 WILD HORSES IS FLYING ALONG, MAINSAIL AND SPINNAKER DRAWING PERFECTLY, IN CLASSIC CARIBBEAN SAILING CONDITIONS.

208-209 *Wild Horses'* bow in an aerial close-up. Here she is flying her asymmetrical spinnaker during the St. Barths Bucket. Although by far the smallest yacht to participate in this prestigious regatta, she consistently finishes with the winners.

210 An aerial view of Wild Horses, taken during the St. Barths Bucket.

210-211 A view from the stern deck aboard Wild Horses. She is continuously maintained in competitive racing form by her owner.

212-213 WILD HORSES REEFED DOWN AND SHOWING OFF HER FORM IN THE BOISTEROUS SEAS OFF ST. BARTHS, RACING IN THE ST. BARTHS BUCKET. THIS PHOTOGRAPH DISPLAYS HER EXCEPTIONALLY GRACEFUL LINES. SHE IS THE LATE JOEL WHITE'S LAST DESIGN.

METEOR

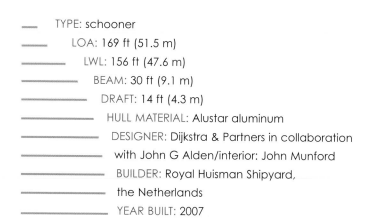

TYPE: schooner

LOA: 169 ft (51.5 m)

LWL: 156 ft (47.6 m)

BEAM: 30 ft (9.1 m)

DRAFT: 14 ft (4.3 m)

HULL MATERIAL: Alustar aluminum

DESIGNER: Dijkstra & Partners in collaboration with John G Alden/interior: John Munford

BUILDER: Royal Huisman Shipyard, the Netherlands

YEAR BUILT: 2007

Anyone who has read *Captains Courageous* or spent any time studying the history of cod fishing can tell you that *Meteor*, lovely as she is, does not look like a Gloucester schooner. And that is no slight on her designers. After all, is there a name more closely associated with schooners than John G. Alden or, for that matter, a designer with credentials for drawing modern classics as impeccable as Gerald Dijkstra?

So let's forego comparisons and consider that *Meteor*, the 169-foot (50 m) schooner launched in 2007 by the Royal Huisman Shipyard, deserves to be admired simply for what she is. For the aesthetically disposed, there is nothing quite as evocative as a time-honored cruising schooner rig with a tall Marconi mainsail and gaff foresail, and here *Meteor* does not disappoint. In fact, she enjoys the best of two worlds: she has all the grace and majesty of a traditional schooner while also affording her owners and crew the unparalleled ease of handling as well as ample safety margins of modern materials and technology.

Meteor's carbon fiber spars and standing rigging are supplied by Rondal, Huisman's proprietary spar and hardware manufacturer, as are her hydraulic winches and all custom fittings. The rest, on deck and below, is classic (if we may be allowed that word in this context) Huisman – that is to say, flawless. John Munford designed the interior, which is a showcase of timeless elegance, and finished the owner and guest accommodations in what has been described as "acres of Swetania mahogany," a light colored tropical wood with a lovely grain.

In a world of modern classic yachts which achieve brilliant performance by adopting modern underwater profiles under their traditional hull profile – fin-and-bulb keels, spade rudders, etc. – Dijkstra has managed a bit of sorcery. Adhering to the owners' request for a comfortable yacht to cruise in, he designed a surprisingly traditional underbody, with a full length keel and attached rudder. What is not surprising is that this configuration produces a sea-kindly motion and directional stability that make *Meteor* a delight to sail in any conditions. Her captain reported sailing in winds gusting over 65 knots in the English Channel with no handling problems of any kind. The sorcery is in her speed. Sailing against J-Class sloops and several other fast megayachts, she won the 2009 St. Barths Bucket Regatta outright and was first in class at the 2010 Newport Bucket. Clearly, her designers have refined the full-length keel concept with no sacrifice in performance.

There is one similarity, however, to those Gloucester schooners: *Meteor's* steering wheel, while not the truly traditional galvanized steel affair that works the rudder through a Simplex worm gear, is properly installed on the forward side of the steering box, with a free-standing binnacle in front. All that's missing are a few dories stacked on deck ...

214-215 THE 169-FOOT (50 M) SCHOONER METEOR IS UNDER FULL SAIL AND WITH A BONE IN HER TEETH IN PERFECT CARIBBEAN CONDITIONS. UNUSUAL FOR A MODERN CLASSIC, SHE HAS A FULL-LENGTH KEEL YET IS CAPABLE OF EXHILARATING SPEED.

216 METEOR BOWLING ALONG PAST ONE OF THE MANY ROCKY "RACING MARKS" AT THE 2010 ST. BARTHS BUCKET REGATTA.

216-217 AN EVOCATIVE PHOTOGRAPH OF METEOR SAILING PAST A LIGHTHOUSE, AS SCHOONERS HAVE BEEN DOING FOR TWO CENTURIES BEFORE HER.

218-219 METEOR IS IN HER ELEMENT: RACING IN THE LORO PIANA SUPERYACHT REGATTA IN A FRESH BREEZE, HERE SHE IS CHASING HER COMPETITION.

ATLANTIC

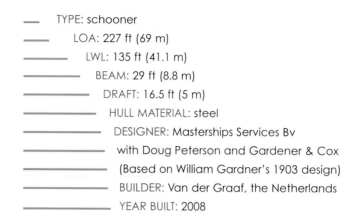

TYPE: schooner
LOA: 227 ft (69 m)
LWL: 135 ft (41.1 m)
BEAM: 29 ft (8.8 m)
DRAFT: 16.5 ft (5 m)
HULL MATERIAL: steel
DESIGNER: Mastersships Services Bv
with Doug Peterson and Gardener & Cox
(Based on William Gardner's 1903 design)
BUILDER: Van der Graaf, the Netherlands
YEAR BUILT: 2008

Twelve days, four hours and one minute from New York Harbor to the Lizard in Southwest England: the mighty schooner *Atlantic's* 1905 record stood for 100 years. With all due respect for *Mari-Cha IV's* achievement in finally beating the record, *Atlantic* did it without the advantages of modern ultralight boatbuilding technology. She was luxuriously appointed below decks and her displacement was 395 tons (360,000 kg), compared to her later rival's 55 tons (50,000 kg). Most importantly, *Atlantic* crossed the ocean without the benefit of modern instant weather reporting. Her skipper, the famous Charlie Barr, simply drove her unrelentingly, at one point ordering owner Wilson Marshall below when Marshall expressed concern at how much sail Barr insisted on carrying.

Ed Kastelein, renowned in sailing circles for his restoration of classic yachts and for building *Eleonora,* the replica of the famous schooner *Westward,* is the man behind the recreation of a new *Atlantic.* Working from the original drawings and specifications of William Gardner, her original designer, naval architect Doug Peterson embraced modern construction techniques (for example, her steel hull is welded and not riveted, as in the first *Atlantic*) while adhering as much as possible to Gardner's design. As part of the quest for authenticity, the spacing of her steel frames has been maintained and custom bronze electric winches, specially manufactured by Harken, replicate the original steam-driven winches.

When she was launched in 1903, *Atlantic* was considered very advanced in her accommodations, even in that era of well-appointed yachts. She boasted electric lights, refrigeration and hot running water. While such amenities nowadays are commonplace in much smaller yachts, at the time they were highly unusual. The replica is luxurious indeed, applying modern technology throughout to provide the greatest degree of comfort possible for a party of up to twelve. It goes without saying that her interior has been finished to the highest standards of joiner work and craftsmanship. Another noticeable difference in accommodations is the fact that while the original yacht sailed with 39 crew housed in what was essentially a bunkhouse forward, modern automated systems have reduced that complement to a crew of 10 – still forward of the mast but in far more comfortable quarters.

Although the original rig had undergone several modifications over the years, for the replica it was decided to adopt the 1905 winning configuration, using aluminum instead of steel for the masts and topmasts and honoring tradition with Sitka spruce booms and gaffs. On deck, *Atlantic* remains a faithful copy of her forebear in the design and arrangement of all deckhouses, hatches, winches and fittings.

Her owner's and builder's insistence on maintaining authenticity wherever possible has made the new *Atlantic* a true modern classic, in some ways more of a reconstruction than a replica. All that's left for her is to beat her own record.

221 *THE RECENTLY LAUNCHED REPLICA OF THE GAFF SCHOONER* ATLANTIC *IS A FAITHFUL REPLICA OF THE YACHT THAT HELD A* TRANSATLANTIC *RECORD SET IN 1905 AND NOT BESTED UNTIL 100 YEARS LATER.*

222-223 ATLANTIC'S *RIG CASTS SHADOWS ON A SUN-DRENCHED SEA. SHE IS AT THE SAME TIME MAJESTIC YET SLENDER AND GRACEFUL, A TRULY BEAUTIFUL SEA GOING YACHT.*

224 THE HELM STATION ABOARD ATLANTIC. THE STEERING WHEEL REMAINS TRUE TO TRADI-
TION AND HAS NO RIM SURROUNDING THE SPOKES. THE BINNACLE IS LIKEWISE A PERFECT
REPLICA OF THE ORIGINAL.

224-225 ATLANTIC'S CREW IS HOISTING HER MAINSAIL. NOTICE THE USE OF TRADITIONAL
WOODEN SHELLED BLOCKS, AN AUTHENTIC AND LOVELY DETAIL.

226-227 THE MASTER STATEROOM BELOW DECKS ON ATLANTIC IS FINISHED IN AN ELEGANT RENDITION OF VINTAGE YACHT INTERIORS, WITH VARNISHED JOINERWORK CONTRASTING THE WHITE BULKHEADS AND OVERHEAD BEAMS.

227 THE CHART STATION DISPLAYS MONITOR ALL SHIP FUNCTIONS AS WELL AS NAVIGATION DISPLAYS.

228-229 *While it is nearly impossible to find fault with any of Atlantic's lines, William Gardner, the naval architect who designed the original boat, drew the perfect spoon bow. This is schooner sailing at its finest!*

REGATTAS

ANTIGUA CLASSIC YACHT REGATTA

VELE D'EPOCA DI IMPERIA

LES RÉGATES ROYALES DE CANNES

MONACO CLASSIC WEEK

LES VOILES DE ST. TROPEZ

Chapter 5

Once someone has lovingly restored a classic, or once an enthusiastic yachtsman has commissioned a replica of a famous yacht, what do they do with her? A logical temptation might be for them to protect their substantial investment and kick back on the yacht club's veranda and watch her swinging idly at her mooring, looking beautiful.

For the slightly more active sailor, there is always the option of going on a leisurely cruise, enjoying the summer breezes and basking in the admiration of the less fortunate who can only gaze enviously from their white plastic sailing craft. There are few things more satisfying than relaxing under a taut, well-rigged awning in a quiet anchorage, sipping a chilled rosé or a rum punch, surrounded by flawlessly varnished mahogany and polished brass, the gaff sails over your head neatly furled inside the lazyjacks.

And then, of course, there's racing.

The premise is a fundamental one, predicated on human nature: when another sailing yacht is in sight, there is no sailor who will not instinctively glance aloft at the set of his canvas and make some minor and probably unnecessary adjustment to his sheets. If the boats get close and are reasonably similar in type, invariably a race ensues. Many, if not most, sailors are honest enough to acknowledge their competitive urges and simply choose to go racing.

Ironically enough, probably the most significant favor handed to owners of classic yachts has been the advance of modern exotic materials. This development in turn has enabled designers and builders to produce boats which, while they may offer exhilarating performance, can only be described as having an idiosyncratic – or perhaps, to be more charitable, purposeful – appearance. As recently as 40 years ago, all sorts of sailing craft would go racing together, with length as the only criterion for de-

termining classes and a rating rule trusted to sort out any disparities. The advent of lightweight and then ultra-lightweight racing boats eventually rendered this approach unworkable. In a relatively short span of time, the hot ocean racers of the wooden boat era were no longer competitive. Clearly, the dear old clunkers needed their own class.

From that point on, the evolution became predictable. The typical regatta format, which originally had included the newfangled modern speed demons as a sort of appendage to the program, inexorably inverted the order of priority and eventually reached the point where the classics, almost as an afterthought, were given a starting gun after the Kevlar sleds had surfed off. But as interest in classic yachts grew, the inevitable next step was the spawning of regattas held exclusively for them.

It started with a few diehards comparing varnish brands and the merits of sawn versus steam bent frames. Racing consisted of sailing around the course trying not to break anything. At some point, as their numbers increased, attempts were made at dividing the boats into a rational and equitable system of classes. It only made sense to separate a gaff-rigged Colin Archer with a maximum speed of four and a half knots from a well-sailed 8 Metre that could easily travel twice as fast.

It should come as no surprise to any sailor familiar with the breed that classic yacht racing started to be, if not exactly competitive, certainly more spirited. And it unquestionably continued to be fun. The rest of the sailing and racing fraternity took note. Pretty soon a few familiar faces from the other, "real" racing world of composites and carbon fiber began to be seen steering or strategizing on board the more competitive yachts. A frequent participant in Mediterranean classic yacht regattas is the flawlessly restored Q-Boat *Cotton Blossom II*, owned and skippered by Dennis Conner of America's Cup fame.

Things started to get serious, which in many ways was a healthy development. Professional sailors were brought on board, especially on the larger boats. Inevitably, the increased competitiveness and professionalism has caused some discreet muttering from the more sporting, not to say relaxed, contestants. While their point of view is certainly understandable, consider the logistics of sailing a 70-foot (20 m) gaff sloop in close company around a racing course, not to mention a 160-foot (50 m) schooner. How many of us even know or can remember how to set a jackyard topsail? Professionals contribute a margin of safety and performance that no transplanted small boat sailor, however enthusiastic, can provide. The classic manifestation of the professional versus amateur question can be found in the history of classic yachts with the 1934 America's Cup, in which *Rainbow* bested *Endeavour*, considered by everyone to be the faster boat. *Rainbow* was sailed by professionals, *Endeavour* by amateur sailors with no big boat experience.

The dear old clunkers have found their own niche and it has become commonplace for a regatta to attract over a hundred classic yachts, from 6-Metre lapstrake cockleshells to majestic gaff schooners and J-Class sloops. They follow a well-established racing circuit, with new venues regularly added. The events have attracted major sponsorships and are professionally organized and managed. Both sides of the North Atlantic have a busy summer schedule while, for obvious reasons, many American and European classic yachts gather in the Caribbean for the winter months. Some classics based in the Caribbean even return the favor, sailing to summer regattas on the American East Coast or the Mediterranean.

The actual events are too numerous to mention in their entirety. The major regattas, typically three- or four-day events, are often connected by feeder races. Thus, after you have finished varnishing your period yacht, you could start in June in Antibes or Porquerolles, where you could acquire your summer stock of rosé, before moving on to Argentario Sailing Week in lovely old Porto Santo Stefano. Cantiere Navale dell'Argentario is located here, featuring the pre-war 12 Metres *Vim* and *Nyala*, as well as the Sparkman & Stephens timeless yawls *Dorade* and *Stormy Weather* – only a few of the many classics restored by their craftsmen.

As the summer unfolds the choice of venues is an embarrassment of riches. There's Vele d'Epoca a Napoli, or the Trophée Bailli de Suffren (a distance race from St. Tropez to Malta), followed by Barcelona Classic Week and Club de Mar Classic Regatta in Palma de Mallorca. To add to the confusion, there is the Trofeo Almirante Conde de Barcelona, which is actually held in Mallorca.

Not surprisingly, all roads lead to that former Roman outpost, St. Tropez, for the season finale. The Vele d'Epoca di Imperia in Italy culminates in an Imperia-Nice feeder race, followed by the Trophée Belle Classe in Nice and the always impressive Régates Royales in Cannes. One more feeder, the Coupe d'Automne du YCF, takes the yachts from Cannes to St. Tropez for Les Voiles de St. Tropez, the last major event of the season.

That's just a sample of the Mediterranean offerings. In England, events like the Brixham Heritage Festival Rally & Race attract sailing trawlers, working boats and all sorts of other classic craft. There is Dartmouth Classic Weekend, a seven-day affair that takes participants from Dartmouth to Paimpol, France, then back to St. Peter Port in Guernsey. Across the English Channel in South Brittany there is La Semaine du Golfe du Morbihan, billed as a maritime festival for traditional and classic boats of all types. Douarnenez and Brest are famous for bringing together traditional working boats. Not to be outdone, Scandinavian countries have joined to create the Scandinavian Classic Yacht Trust to promote classic yacht regattas and events.

North American classics enjoy similar variety.

Some events, like the Eggemoggin Reach Regatta, are perhaps more local in flavor but still generate great enthusiasm. Many competitors can be found at the more encompassing events, such as the Corinthian Classic Yacht Regatta at Marblehead in Massachusetts, the Opera House Cup in Nantucket and the Museum of Yachting Classic Yacht Regatta at Newport, Rhode Island. Less heralded but no less classic are the many one-design fleets found at countless yacht clubs, racing boats like the Winter Harbor one-designs that date to 1908. Starling Burgess' 1929 Atlantic creations, the Wianno Seniors (popular in Nantucket Sound) and fleets of International One-Designs on both coasts all can be seen actively racing and are lovingly maintained.

Cold weather causes any sailor worth his or her salt to head south for the Caribbean. The premier event for classics, the Antigua Classic Yacht Regatta, has been a fixture since 1987, attracting huge gaff schooners, J-Class sloops and classic yachts of every size and rig, including traditional local sloops built on remote island beaches. Its inclusiveness has made it an obligatory rendezvous for European and American yachts of all stripes. It has also inspired several other similar events, such as the St. Maarten Classics and the Grenada Classic Yacht Regatta.

All this racing can seem overwhelming, and if you really wanted to campaign your lovely classic and seriously follow the circuit you would barely have time to touch up the varnish, much less find a quiet moment under that perfectly set awning. Just the logistics of getting her from one port to the next and finding a crew that understands how to properly peak your gaff when sailing upwind, not to mention more mundane details like feeding that crew, can become daunting. It is then that racing classics can start to feel suspiciously similar to racing those Kevlar sleds.

Nevertheless, classic boat racing in all of its manifestations manages to keep both feet firmly on the deck. A significant difference you will notice between races held for modern boats and those held for classic yachts takes place at the dock after the finish gun. The sleds after their race lie at the dock empty, their crews ashore seeking comfort. The classics, on the other hand, are alive, with crews lingering aboard fussing with small chores, enjoying a tot of rum or standing on the dock gazing fondly at their boat. As passionate and competitive as the owners, skippers and crews may be, there is always a camaraderie and a shared sense of personal fulfillment derived from a job well done.

Racing a classic yacht – never mind the arduous and often expensive process of restoring and maintaining her – is indeed a responsibility. Most owners consider themselves to be caretakers, a role which entails not only making sure that their cherished charge is kept in the best possible condition but that she be sailed and enjoyed and used as originally intended. After all, not many sailors have Nat Herreshoff, William Fife or Olin Stephens looking over their shoulder, making sure their boats are sailed as they were meant to be.

Bringing back these classics and taking them racing has been a long and sometimes arduous process.

After their early years of sailing with cotton sails and manila lines, with perhaps a sextant to keep them going when out of sight of land, so many were neglected and left, like Manon Lescaut in Puccini's opera, "sola, perduta, abbandonata" (alone, lost, abandoned). It makes quite a story, the change in perspective that led to the rescue of so many boats from Caribbean mangroves, boat yard back lots and mud banks. It is more than just the boats that have been rescued – the craftsmanship required to repair, rebuild and re-rig them has been rediscovered as well, surely a valuable treasury of skills requiring not only precision but also patience. Racing these classics in so many ways has brought back a more sportsmanlike attitude to the sport, a sense of enjoyment of the moment for its own sake, and damn that extra tenth of a knot. They have come quite a ways, those dear old clunkers.

REGATTAS

ANTIGUA CLASSIC
YACHT REGATTA

234 *THE J-CLASS YACHTS* RANGER, CAMBRIA *AND* VELSHEDA *RACING OFF* FALMOUTH HARBOR, ANTIGUA, *IN HOT PURSUIT OF THE SCHOONER* WINDROSE *AT THE* 2004 ANTIGUA CLASSIC YACHT REGATTA.

234-235 RANGER *IS LEADING* WINDROSE, VELSHEDA *AND* CAMBRIA *(REEFED DOWN) DURING THE THIRD RACE OF THE* 2004 ANTIGUA CLASSIC YACHT REGATTA.

236-237 BIG BOAT RACING IS BORN AGAIN! THE SCHOONER WINDROSE AND THE J-CLASS YACHTS RANGER AND VELSHEDA REVELING IN THE TRADE WINDS AT CLOSE QUARTERS.

238-239 THE CREW IS DOUSING THE TOPSAIL ON A TRADITIONAL SCHOONER DURING THE 2006 ANTIGUA CLASSIC YACHT REGATTA.

239 THE COMPLEX RUNNING RIGGING ON OLDER SCHOONERS REQUIRES CONSTANT TENDING. HERE A CREW MEMBER CLIMBS ALOFT TO CLEAR AS SNAG.

240-241 ACTION AT CLOSE QUARTERS – VELSHEDA, TO THE RIGHT, CUTS INSIDE RANGER AT THE LEEWARD MARK. SHE WAS LATER PENALIZED FOR THIS DANGEROUS MANEUVER.

241 RANGER AND VELSHEDA ARE ROUNDING THE LEEWARD MARK DURING THEIR MATCH RACE ON DAY FOUR OF THE 2004 ANTIGUA CLASSIC YACHT REGATTA.

242-243 LATER IN THE SAME MATCH RACE, RANGER (NEAR CAM-
ERA) AND VELSHEDA ARE REACHING ALONG AT HULL SPEED WITHIN
A BOAT LENGTH OF EACH OTHER. THEY WERE NEVER MORE THAN
100 YARDS (90 M) APART FOR THE ENTIRE 25-MILE COURSE.

VELE D'EPOCA DI IMPERIA

244 THE CLASSIC YACHT FLEET JUST AFTER THE START. OBVIOUSLY, TRADITION IS SOMETIMES IGNORED IN THE HEAT OF ACTION, JUDGING BY THE NUMBER OF MODERN ASYMMETRICAL SPINNAKERS FLYING.

245 MARISKA AND ORION RACING AT CLOSE QUARTERS DURING THE VELE D'EPOCA DI IMPERIA. BOTH YACHTS AND THEIR CREWS ARE CLEARLY ENJOYING THE BREEZY CONDITIONS.

246-247 TUIGA IS AHEAD AND TO LEEWARD OF MOONBEAM IV *WHILE RACING AT THE 2008 VELE D'EPOCA DI IMPERIA. THE CONDITIONS ARE WINDY ENOUGH TO PREVENT THEM FROM SETTING TOPSAILS.*

LES RÉGATES ROYALES DE CANNES

248 *Les Régates Royales, Cannes, 2006. Moonbeam IV and Orion split tacks under the fort, sailing in light air.*

249 *The gaff schooner Eleanora leads the J-Class Cambria on a windy beat at Les Régates Royales. Both yachts are about to change headsails, as evidenced by their crews clustered on the foredeck.*

250-251 Sailing as a spectator sport – two competitors battling near shore at Les Régates Royales, Cannes, on September 30, 2007, provide a spectacular sight from the beach.

251 Light air action under the ramparts of the fort, during the Prada Challenge for Classic Yachts, Cannes, 2003.

252-253 *JUST AFTER THE START AT THE 2007 RÉGATES ROYALES DE CANNES, THE COMPETITORS ARE FIGHTING FOR POSITION ON A BRISK STARBOARD TACK.*

MONACO
CLASSIC WEEK

254   RACING DURING THE TUIGA CENTENARY CELEBRATION AT THE 2009 MONACO CLASSIC WEEK.

254-255   THREE COMPETITORS ARE IN NEAR-PERFECT ALIGNMENT AS THEY GHOST ALONG UNDER FULL SAIL UNDER THE DRAMATIC MONACO SHORELINE.

256-257 *THE RACING FLEET LIES BECALMED WAITING FOR THE SEA BREEZE IN FRONT OF MONACO HARBOR, WITH EVERY POSSIBLE SCRAP OF CANVAS SET TO CATCH ANY RANDOM PUFF OF AIR.*

258-259 *WHEN THE WIND FINALLY FILLS IN, THE SAILING BECOMES EXHILARATING. NOTE THE QUADRILATERAL JIB, A SAIL VERY RARELY SEEN TODAY, ON THE BOAT TO LEEWARD.*

260-261 *ON BOARD THE J-CLASS YACHT CAMBRIA, CHASING THE COMPETITION ON A PORT TACK BEAT.*

LES VOILES DE
ST. TROPEZ

262 THE STARTING LINE AT THE 2000 VOILES DE ST. TROPEZ, SEEN FROM THE TOP OF THE HILL. LES VOILES INCLUDES MODERN AS WELL AS CLASSIC YACHTS IN SEVERAL CLASSES.

262-263 AT THE 2008 VOILES DE ST. TROPEZ, TWO CLASSIC YACHTS MANEUVER FOR POSITION IN VERY TIGHT QUARTERS. ST. TROPEZ'S CHARACTERISTIC YELLOW BELL TOWER IS IN THE BACKGROUND.

264-265 ON BOARD THE MAJESTIC GAFF SCHOONER ELEANORA, LEADING TWO OTHER GAFF SCHOONERS IN 2004.

265 THE WILLIAM FIFE CLASSIC MOONBEAM IV SAILING ON PORT TACK UNDER A LOWERING SKY.

266 PETITE LANDE AND LELANTINA, COMPETING IN THE 2003 VOILES DE ST. TROPEZ.

267 THE BEAUTIFULLY RESTORED WILLIAM FIFE CUTTERS MOONBEAM IV AND MARIQUITA, PHOTOGRAPHED DURING LES VOILES DE ST. TROPEZ IN OCTOBER 2007.

268-269 THE REASON WHY SAILORS LOVE RACING CLASSIC YACHTS – LULWORTH, MOONBEAM IV AND MARIQUITA SAILING NECK-AND-NECK. IT LOOKS LIKE LULWORTH COULD USE A LONGER BOWSPRIT!

ACKNOWLEDGMENTS

I have had a lifelong fascination with classic yachts. Naturally there are many reasons one becomes smitten with classics: they are drop-dead gorgeous to look at, they are exhilarating to sail and they evoke a sense not only of history but also of mystery. In the last couple of decades there has been a resurgence in yacht restoration – a desire to preserve the past. At the same time, there has been a trend to build modern classics honoring designs from the golden age of yachting, but building in new materials and utilizing modern technology.   Ongoing events and regattas around the world keep classic yachts alive and thriving. Classic yachts will never go out of style!

I could not have written this book without the invaluable assistance of my long-time friend and colleague, Alessandro Vitelli. Sandro took me on a memorable sail on a lovely Hinckley yawl Down East in Maine in the 1970s. He is an ace sailor, an aficionado of all things classic, an amateur historian, and he has a marvelous perspective on yachting from all eras. Sandro was my go-to source for all discussions about the yachts that appear in this book.

The Publisher would like to thank for their helpful collaboration: Ed Kastelein and Sophie Kastelein, Joseph Artese Design, Andre Hoek and Koos Goris (Hoek Design), Eva Meijer (Hoek Brokerage), Jurjen van't Verlaat (Royal Huisman), Bruce Johnson (Sparkman & Stephens), Anneliek van der Linde (Dijkstra & Partners Naval Architects), Jill Hayward (International Dragon Association), Captain Herbert J. Motley (Dashing Rock), Patrick Gifford and Jill Hayward (International Dragon Association), Robert Pijselman.

INDEX

PHOTO CREDITS

page 1 Guido Cantini/Kos/SeaSee.com
pages 2-3 Kos/SeaSee.com
pages 4-5 Carlo Borlenghi/rolex/
  SeaSee.com
pages 6-7 Cory Silken
pages 8-9 Carlo Borlenghi/SeaSee.com
page 11 Gilles Martin - Raget/SeaSee.com
page 12 Marc de Tienda/SeaSee.com
pages 20-21 Carlo Borlenghi/SeaSee.com
pages 22-23 Cory Silken
pages 24-25 Gilles Martin-Raget/
  SeaSee.com
pages 28-29 Library of Congress/Prints &
  Photographs Division/Detroit Publishing
  Company Collection/LC-D4-62271
pages 30-31 Library of Congress/Prints &
  Photographs Division/Detroit Publishing
  Company Collection/LC-D4-62270 DLC
page 31 Library of Congress/Prints &
  Photographs Division/Detroit Publishing
  Company Collection/LC-D4-21980 DLC
page 32 Christian Février/Bluegreen
page 33 Bettmann/Corbis
pages 34-35 Library of Congress/Prints &
  Photographs Division/Detroit Publishing
  Company Collection/LC-D421635
page 36 Library of Congress/Prints &
  Photographs Division/Detroit Publishing
  Company Collection/LC-D4-21722
page 37 Christian Février/Bluegreen
page 38 Library of Congress/Prints &
  Photographs Division/Detroit Publishing
  Company Collection/LC-D4-21754 DLC
pages 38-39 Library of Congress/Prints &
  Photographs Division/Detroit Publishing
  Company Collection/LC-D4-21773 DLC
pages 42-43 Akg-Images/
  PhotoserviceElecta
page 44 Hulton Archive/Getty Images
pages 44-45 Hulton-Deutsch Collection/
  Corbis
page 46 Library of Congress/Prints &
  Photographs Division/Detroit Publishing
  Company Collection/LC-D4-5371 DLC
page 47 Bettmann/Corbis
pages 48-49 Christian Février/Bluegreen
pages 50-51 Erwan Quémére /Bluegreen
page 52 Gilles Martin-Raget/SeaSee.com
page 53 Gilles Martin-Raget/SeaSee.com
pages 54-55 Philip Plisson/SeaSee.com
page 55 Le Corre Nicolas/Gamma/
  Eyedea Presse/Contrasto
pages 56-57 Christian Février/Bluegreen
pages 58-59 Carlo Borlenghi/SeaSee.com
pages 60-61 Carlo Borlenghi/SeaSee.com
page 61 left Carlo Borlenghi/SeaSee.com
page 61 right Carlo Borlenghi/SeaSee.com
pages 62-63 Guillaume Plisson/SeaSee.com
pages 64-65 Rick Tomlinson/SeaSee.com
pages 66-67 Philip Plisson/SeaSee.com
page 68 top Gilles Martin-Raget/
  SeaSee.com
page 68 bottom Guido Cantini/SeaSee.com
pages 68-69 Marc de Tienda/SeaSee.com
page 70 Guillaume Plisson/SeaSee.com
page 71 Guillaume Plisson/SeaSee.com
pages 72-73 Thierry Seray/SeaSee.com

page 74 Cory Silken
pages 76-77 Cory Silken
pages 78-79 Cory Silken
page 81 Gary John Norman/Bluegreen
pages 82-83 Carlo Borlenghi/SeaSee.com
page 84 Carlo Borlenghi/SeaSee.com
pages 84-85 Onne van der Wal/Bluegreen
pages 86-87 Carlo Borlenghi/SeaSee.com
page 87 left Carlo Borlenghi/SeaSee.com
page 87 right Carlo Borlenghi/SeaSee.com
pages 88-89 Guido Cantini/SeaSee.com
page 89 Rick Tomlinson/Bluegreen
page 90 Cory Silken
page 92 Christian Fevrier/Bluegreen
pages 92-93 Cory Silken
pages 94-95 Guy Gurney/SeaSee.com
page 98 Imagno/Getty Images
pages 100-101 Carlo Borlenghi/
  SeaSee.com
pages 102-103 Carlo Borlenghi/
  SeaSee.com
page 103 Carlo Borlenghi/SeaSee.com
pages 104-105 Guillaume Plisson/
  SeaSee.com
pages 106-107 Tim Wright/Kos/
  SeaSee.com
pages 108-109 Gilles Martin-Raget/
  SeaSee.com
pages 110-11 Gilles Martin-Raget/
  SeaSee.com
page 111 Gilles Martin-Raget/
  SeaSee.com
pages 112-113 Christian Février/Bluegreen
page 113 Gilles Martin-Raget/
  SeaSee.com
pages 114-115 Christian Février/Bluegreen
pages 116-117 Christian Février/Bluegreen
page 118 Guillaume Plisson/SeaSee.com
pages 118-119 Guillaume Plisson/
  SeaSee.com
page 121 Keystone-France/Getty Images
page 122 Imagno/Austrian Archives/
  Archivio Alinari, Firenze
pages 124-125 Rick Tomlinson/Bluegreen
page126 Keystone-France/Getty Images
page 127 New York Daily News
  Archive/Getty Images
page 128 Dijkstra & Partners Naval
  Architects
page 129 Ingrid Abery /Bluegreen
pages 130-131 Guillaume Plisson/
  SeaSee.com
page 133 Ajax News/SeaSee.com
page 134 Ajax News/SeaSee.com
pages 134-135 Ajax News/SeaSee.com
pages 136-137 Cory Silken
page 138 Christophe Launay/SeaSee.com
page 139 Carlo Borlenghi/SeaSee.com
page 140 Tim Wright/Photoaction.com
page 141 Cory Silken
page 143 Philip Plisson/SeaSee.com
pages 144-145 Fox Photos/Stringer/Getty
  Images
pages 146-147 A. Hudson /Stringer/Getty
  Images
page 148 Keystone-France/Getty
  Images

page 149 Keystone-France/Getty
  Images
page 150 Christian Février/Bluegreen
page 151 Christian Février/Bluegreen
pages 152-153 Christian Février/Bluegreen
pages 154-155 Christian Février/Bluegreen
pages 156-157 Carlo Borlenghi/
  SeaSee.com
page 157 Christian Février/Bluegreen
pages 158-159 Gilles Martin-Raget/
  SeaSee.com
page 159 Carlo Borlenghi/SeaSee.com
page 160 Keystone-France/Getty Images
page 162 Christian Février/Bluegreen
page 163 Dijkstra & Partners Naval
  Architect
page 165 Bettmann/Corbis
page 166-167 Cory Silken
page 168 top Royal Huisman Shipyard BV
page 168 bottom Royal Huisman
  Shipyard BV
page 169 Cory Silken
pages 170-171 Cory Silken
page 171 Cory Silken
page 172 Cory Silken
page 173 Cory Silken
page 174 Cory Silken
page 175 Cory Silken
pages 176-177 Onne van der Wal/
  Bluegreen
pages 178-179 Keystone-France/Getty
  Images
page 179 Keystone-France/Getty Images
pages 180-181 Onne van der Wal/
  Bluegreen
pages 182-183 Carlo Borlenghi/Kos/
  SeaSee.com
page 183 left Carlo Borlenghi/Kos/
  SeaSee.com
page 183 right Carlo Borlenghi/Kos/
  SeaSee.com
pages 184-185 Kos/SeaSee.com
page 187 Hoek Design Naval Architects BV
page 188 Hoek Design Naval Architects BV
page 189 Hoek Design Naval Architects BV
page 192 Cory Silken
pages 194-195 Cory Silken
pages 196-197 Neil Rabinowitz/Bluegreen
pages 198-199 Tim Wright/Photoaction.com
pages 200-201 Dana Jinkins
page 201 top Dana Jinkins
page 201 center Dana Jinkins
pages 202-203 Tim Wright/Photoaction.com
page 204 Rick Tomlinson/Bluegreen
pages 206-207 Cory Silken
pages 208-209 Cory Silken
page 210 Tim Wright/Photoaction.com
pages 210-211 Cory Silken
pages 212-213 Cory Silken
pages 214-215 Tim Wright/Photoaction.com
page 216 Tim Wright/Photoaction.com
pages 216-217 Andrea Pisapia/
  SeaSee.com
pages 218-219 Cory Silken
page 221 Gilles Martin-Raget/SeaSee.com
page 222 Gilles Martin-Raget/SeaSee.com
page 223 Kees Stuip

page 224 Kees Stuip
pages 224-225 Gilles Martin-Raget/
  SeaSee.com
pages 226-227 Kees Stuip
page 227 Kees Stuip
pages 228-229 Kees Stuip
page 234 Onne van der Wal/Bluegreen
page 234-235 Carlo Borlenghi/Kos/
  SeaSee.com
pages 236-237 Onne van der Wal/
  Bluegreen
pages 238-239 Daniel Forster/SeaSee.com
page 239 Daniel Forster/SeaSee.com
pages 240-241 Onne van der Wal/
  Bluegreen
page 241 Carlo Borlenghi/Kos/
  SeaSee.com
pages 242-243 Carlo Borlenghi/
  SeaSee.com
page 244 James Robinson Taylor/
  SeaSee.com
page 245 Davide Marcesini/SeaSee.com
pages 246-247 Paolo Tonato/SeaSee.com
page 248 Guido Cantini/SeaSee.com
page 249 Cory Silken
pages 250-251 Ingrid Abery/Bluegreen
page 251 Guido Cantini/SeaSee.com
pages 252-253 Gilles Martin-Raget/
  SeaSee.com
page 254 Kos/SeaSee.com
pages 254-255 Bruno Cocozza/
  SeaSee.com
pages 256-257 Philip Plisson/SeaSee.com
pages 258-259 Kos/SeaSee.com
pages 260-261 Bruno Cocozza/
  SeaSee.com
page 262 Carlo Borlenghi/SeaSee.com
page 262-263 James Robinson Taylor/
  SeaSee.com
pages 264-265 Kos/SeaSee.com
page 265 Guilain Grenier/SeaSee.com
pages 266 Sergio Dionisio/SeaSee.com
page 267 Th.Martinez/SeaSee.com
pages 268-269 Th.Martinez/SeaSee.com

WHITE STAR PUBLISHERS

WS White Star Publishers®
is a registered trademark property
of Edizioni White Star s.r.l.

© 2011 Edizioni White Star s.r.l.
Via Candido Sassone, 24
13100 Vercelli, Italy
www.whitestar.it

Editing: Schaefer John

All rights reserved. No part of this publication
may be reproduced, stored in a retrieval
system or transmitted in any form or
by any means, electronic, mechanical,
photocopying, recording or otherwise,
without written permission from the publisher.

ISBN 978-88-544-0580-6
1 2 3 4 5 6   15 14 13 12 11

Printed in Italy